The Bl
New Fiction, Poetry
Issue 43 | A

The Blue Nib

New Fiction, Poetry, Essays and Reviews
Loughshinny, Skerries. Co. Dublin Ireland.
Info@thebluenib.com

Publisher Dave Kavanagh
Reviews Editor: Emma Lee
Write Life Editor: Clare Morris
Poetry Editors: Tracy Gaughan, Denise O'Hagan,
Felicia McCarthy, Clara Burghelea

© Copyright remains with the authors, 2020
Cover Illustration by Pixabay

ISBN 978-1-8381041-5-3

The Blue Nib gratefully acknowledges the support of our subscribers without whom this publication would be impossible.

Contents

Abhaile
Poetry from Ireland and the UK
with Tracy Gaughan

Editorial	1
Poetry by George Szirtes	3
Poetry by Mark Roper	6
Poetry by Eleanor Hooker	10
Poetry by Luke Kennard	15

North America Time
Poetry from the USA and Canada
with Felicia McCarthy

Editorial	19
Poetry by Mary Oishi	21
Poetry by Carolyn Martin	22
Poetry by Adina Dabija	24
Poetry by Jeff Santosuosso	26
Poetry by Pui Ying Wong	28

The Big Interview

Michael Morpurgo in conversation with Clare Morris	32

The Write Life with Clare Morris

A Writerly Alchemy	51
The Alchemy of Words by Sophia Kouidou-Giles	54
Tsundoku and the Art of Infinite Reading by Michael Paul Hogan	55
Alchemical salad by Dominic Fisher	58
Questions and Answers by Kevin Kling	61

International Poets & Poetry in Translation
with Clara Burghelea

Editorial	63
Poetry by Cătălina Florina Florescu	65
Poetry by Josie Di Sciascio-Andrews	68
Poetry by Margot Saffer	70
Poetry by Viviana Fiorentino	72

The Critical Nib with Emma Lee

Editorial	75
Jacob Ross's *Black Rain Falling*,	76
Bhanu Kapil's *How to Wash a Heart*	78
Nathaneal O'Reilly's *(Un) Belonging*	81

Seanchaí Short Fiction

Haus des Meeres by Antony Osgood	84
Carousel by Helen Campbell	91
Jumpers by Delia Pring	95

An Astráil
Poetry from Australia and New Zealand
with Denise O'Hagan

Editorial	106
Featured Poet Peter Boyle	108
Poetry by Kate McNamara	110
Poetry by Davide Angelo	112
Poetry by Julie Maclean	114
Contributors in order of appearance	116

Dedicated to the memory of James (Jay) Patterson with whom I had many conversations about writing and with whom I shared many unique stories.

Abhaile:
Poetry from Ireland and the UK
with Tracy Gaughan

Editorial

This issue features poetry from Ireland's Eleanor Hooker and Mark Roper, *Next Generation Poet* Luke Kennard, and work, including in translation, from Hungarian-born British poet George Szirtes. We enjoy reading poetry because every time we enter a poem we become somebody else. To paraphrase Edward Hirsh, poems breathe meaning into our lives, and with our own knowledge horizons, we breathe life into poems. As readers we have this responsibility, to mutually participate in language.

George Szirtes is a poet alive in language. His intelligent verse renews and reaffirms its capacity to move us, and from his emotionally powerful search for truth, that *plain tongue explaining plainness to itself* in an increasingly controlled world: *the day I died/they made it perfectly clear/that I had not died*, to the *unintended repercussions* of Luke Kennard's reasons for seasons, to Mark Roper's recollections of *all the dear dead/does their presence rise* - this collection is charged with meaning and remembrance. On these pages are poems of tenderness and human understanding. Poems full of flux and possibility that prod, provoke, and open up the senses. It is my pleasure to introduce them to you.

I was struck by Eleanor Hooker's archipelago of poems with a bee motif. The poet's bent to *wheedle with words* is a gift from a bee who tasted her lip in the crib. Bees in myth were prescient messengers believed to bridge worlds. And from each poet's domain, a communiqué that nothing is black or white but that life, in the words of Louis MacNeice, *is a mad weir of tigerish waters/a prism of delight and pain.* Hooker enters those wild waters of history to re-inhabit *the gloom* but re-emerges too late. With *terror already visited,* a poet's task is one of ethical remembrance - to give voice to the voiceless victims of life unjust and unfair. From the prism of pain comes a message of hope in Szirtes' poem for a sick friend. As a self unselfs *the sea is dark but here and there the light/ catches the waves even at dead of night.* Luke Kennard's surreal and illuminating narratives link the philosophical and the sensual: *I would also like my skin to be thought.* There are dualities in personality and poetry, *some things are just between you and yourself, but to write is to hurl a part of yourself towards* someone; to turn your private possessions into images as Heaney would say. And in these prose poems, as in Szirtes' images, time flourishes exposing falsities and truths, teasing us into resyncing and returning (particularly in this period of puzzledom) to that post-Gregorian year that *was only 282 days long.* And latterly a message of delight from Irish poet Mark Roper. The broad-leafed beauty in his poetry hails our interconnectedness with nature that dwells in us as we live in it: *The house takes place on bog,* he says, *the cast of bees in your studio.* Bees bridging worlds and poems.

There is a communality to poetry that links us as readers. In these solitary and isolating times, this particular collection I hope will leave us feeling less alone and more connected. To borrow from Hooker, poetry is *still here, praying the old prayers.* My sincere thanks to George Szirtes, Eleanor Hooker, Mark Roper, and Luke Kennard for their enriching contributions to this issue.

Tracy Gaughan
IRL/UK Poetry Editor

Poetry by George Szirtes

ABACUS

Listen to the rain
counting out your works and days
on its abacus.

How neatly it plots
each hour. How precise it is!
Set the clock by it,

there is still time. Rain
will leave you tender margins
to scrawl your name in.

A MYRIAD SHARDS

In the land of a myriad shards
there is a word that glistens.
It is the plain tongue explaining
		plainness to itself,
slowly, deliberately, as fully as it can.

But what it loves, it loves: it loves
		soft moon, hard stars,
the great green splayed nature of a thing
that can be told like this,
in this voice, among shards, however many,
		however myriad, under however many hard stars.

AFTER

On the day I died
they made it perfectly clear
that I had not died.

Nobody had died.
It was there in the records
that we had not died.

It was consoling.
We celebrated the fact,
or would have done so

had we been alive.

OCEAN
for Karen Redman

The utter misery of hanging in
when all you need is one shot and it's past;
the wretchedness of living in your skin
when you could scatter in one silent blast.
You see confusion in the panicked eye
and enter it as if you were a ghost
before you've even had a chance to die.
The dreary ocean lapping at your coast
has not yet swallowed you but here you are,
a self unselfing, a mind letting go
its hard-acquired armour, avatar
to a being you once had claims to know.
The sea is dark but here and there the light
catches the waves even at dead of night.

from the Hungarian of Anna Szabó
MY SON'S FIRST PHOTOGRAPH

Unter den Linden, the even light aslant
My little boy and I are in the street,
He seeing, feeling, sniffing and touching the skin
Of the city – it is its bones I've come to greet.

The dead live here. They're simply everywhere
Their monuments pulse through the Berlin air,
Beating at the pavement in a dream.
The great wall's shadow falls across the ground
That you can cross as you would a stream.

A four year old's awareness is still dim
The blank gaze is too natural to him.
For him no corpse, no wartime episode
But pixels of light on an endless road.

Can I take a picture? I bend down to his height,
And snap he takes a shot of me
A moment and it's done. Preserved in light.

Poetry by Mark Roper

OPEN HOUSE

The house takes place on bog.
When the milk lorry goes by,
our rooms are gently shaken.

~

Unseen, unheard, each autumn
thousands of clusterflies
slip somehow into the attic
to sleep away the winter.

A sunny day sees a dozen
seep through the ceiling
to grieve the golden windows.

~

A spider's listening device
in every dark corner,
roads known only to ants;

woollens coddling moths,
worms adding their code
to the words of our books;

springtail and silverfish,
dark-winged fungus gnat;
beetles eating the carpet,

dust mites feasting
on cranefly fuselage,
on flakes of our skin.

~

The cast of bees
in your studio
after the funeral,

which led to finding
the colony of bats
inside the fascia,

which led to the bat
which entered
the bedroom last thing

where it described
in its own good time
circle after circle

IN THE BLEAK MIDWINTER

What shall I give him, poor as I am?

I've sung these words for so many years,
but each time it gets harder,
until now I cannot sing them for tears.

If I were a shepherd, I would bring a lamb.

Is it I first sang them long, long ago
in my father's church, snowlight
silvering the walls, snow on snow on snow?

If I were a wise man, I would do my part.

All the long gone lives, all the dear dead,
does their presence rise to close
my throat, to soak the eyes in my head?

Yet what I can I give him, give my heart.

Might it all come down to that last word –
how the heart, if ungiven,
weeps, where once it sang like a bird?

COMING OUT

Like birds on the brink
of a nest, unfledged,
beaks agape, there we were,
on the Mauma Road,
between Coumaraglin Mountain
and a far-off, shining sea.

Out of house, out of hedge
we were there,
larksong running
in stations of air,
soft heads of bog cotton
nodding assent to it all.

Words, what were they, and how
should we use them?

The coming of evening
over ridge and valley,
dewfall of stars
in the endless dark –
would we ever again
be ready, be able for this?

Poetry by Eleanor Hooker

SELF-PORTRAIT IN A HONEYBEE'S EYE

In the version my mother tells,
one hung in the still air, hummed
above my crib, its saddlebags
yellow laden. She shooed it,
she says, but not before
it tasted my lip. And that is why,
my mother says, I am chosen
to wheedle with words.

I recall its curved fur, and my infant
reflection repeated in its compound
eyes, how it hung in the air, still,
above me. And when it landed,
the secrets that tumbled from its
saddlebag drove into my lip,
and that is why I speak messages
from the otherworld to this.

It is why, when in my honeybee coat
you cannot know me, but grasp the sting
deep inside me may eventually kill me.
And as I tremble from flower to disguise,
lost in a copse of words, I hum who I am.

from **TRACES**

V

particle

With neither a window nor door
to admit particles of light,
this darkened room
has a gargoyle
shadowing the cornice,
and when the room tilts,
you fall past one another,
changing places.
You call out to any who
might hear - *I am here*
I am still here, praying the old prayers.

RETURNING TO THE LAND OF THE DEAD
for Eileen Mary Warburton Biggs

I daub my face and arms with vodka –
an old gardener's trick, so mosquitos
leave off their blood-fest. Balanced
on a tap of touch and turn, against
the hand-cranked grinding wheel,
the slash-hook whets for the cut.

Along the foreshore, an August breeze
plays water music, tender, through
each reed. I swing and find my rhythm,
and as the thicket of brambles unpuzzle,
what was once hidden is now in sight.
I feel the first stings on my eyelids,

my lips, my hands. I tug at my shirt –
wasps cling to my breasts, back, belly.
Before the lake closes above me, I see
the nest –a parchment ball sliced
to reveal deep chambers, its darkest
secrets. I swim through the gloom –

disturb a pike perfecting toothy menace,
follow launching rails for *Vanya*
to the end of the pier, where I break
surface a century earlier. As aspens brustle
and grebe calls bump the quiet,
I test my voice and it returns an echo,

sounding time's inevitability.
This vintage summer wears long
linen skirts and high lace collars,
but is not naïve, indifferent or plain.
In the orchard I stand beneath a fruit tree,
breathe a familiar fermenting scent,

watch five drunken wasps devour a plum,
tear at its bruised and broken flesh –
in greed lies savagery. One wasp hovers
at eye level, daring me to flinch,
but recognizing a fighter, and my stone-cold
intention should it strike, it returns to its feasting.

I feel your eyes on me, Eileen, know you
have seen me before and are not afraid.
Time exists in a loop here, where past
and future are open corridors. You wait
by the door to the rose garden, your face
in shadow under your straw hat, but I see

how you smile at my dishevelled ghost –
a scrap of endurance newly emerged
from the lake. There is no warning
I can signal, for already you are lost,
terror already visited, but having found
you here, I will bring something of you back.

HIVE
    after Les Murray

I am the hive
that broods and yields,
I am the dance
of honey and nectar,
I am an apiary,
a colony in disorder–
spring dwindle
and autumn collapse.
I am the hum
from moulded mud,
a nest on high
ground near rain.
I am storm clouds
that climb the air,
that anvil
and strike,
and strike
the troposphere.
I am storm clouds
that burst
and spill un-goodly
psalms–
of end time,
of bees and keepers.
When *neonics*
grip bees
in a deadly waltz,
and pledge
to money
our share
of the crop –
gain is already decline,
is declension,
is descent and decay.
I am earth nurse
and centre–
the colony
that swarms and leaves,
a flight of honey and nectar.

Poetry by Luke Kennard

Poems from *'Notes on the Sonnets'* to be published April 2021 by Penned in the Margins

3

Without meaning to we're taking photos of each other taking photos of each other again. We're outside the kitchen window getting high around a tin table until all I can talk about is a Rubik's cube where every face is made of another smaller Rubik's cube, but it would only work if they're spheres. Then I get quite agitated and demand someone fetches me the pepper grinder because of the terpenoids, and I like the way the word terpenoids feels in my mouth so much I just keep saying it, *terpenoids terpenoids terpenoids*. Unblessed in the evening air, unblessed. There's such an obsession with wrinkles sonnets 1-74 it's as if the whole sequence had been commissioned by a luxury skin care salve. I don't know about you, but I didn't have children so that they'd *look* like me; it feels weird even having to point that out. Although, you say, head cocked, reflected in the window I just photographed the people photographing themselves through, it's actually quite important being pretty, isn't it? More than we care to admit? I like having attractive friends. I laugh because you do. That's a low-key outrageous thing to say. No it's not. Anyway, everyone's attractive. There is a warmth in just leaning against the windowsill with you I'd like to revisit. I won't.

46

Moiety: two parts. Taxation. In property law, for instance, you own half your maisonette and lease the other half from someone else. The moiety in your brother's eye. Some molecules are water-loving. Some molecules are water-fearing. In anthropology moiety means one of two distinct groups within a tribe.

I interned as an interloper and now I care / about things which should not concern me, broke the key off in the lock, spent the deposit. Here are the two parts of your country, here are the two distinct tribes within each half, here are... In French it just means *half*. In theology you own one of your eyes and the other belongs to God.

37

The way hangovers mature, in your 30s, into a kind of existential mould. I want the kind of success and happiness for you I want for my own children. I want you to feel loved and known or known and loved or, failing that, because really who can expect such extravagance, I want the ache to be transfigured into something you can use. Otherwise, knowing that you exist, that at this moment you are waiting for a train, that you have had to start the same page again because you weren't concentrating, that you are tired, that if someone asked you something they would get to hear your voice. I love the channels dammed with exhausting half-thoughts. Funny how the *latte* has become one of the laziest class signifiers, as if every dead high-street didn't contain at least two Costas.

17

We're mixing gin with lemon Fanta and talking about the problem with posterity, about which we all have our own ideas whilst harbouring secret desires for a *Collected* in ten, twenty, thirty years' time. Nobody wants to admit to being part of the problem because believing that you are part of the problem is profoundly uncomfortable. Also some things are just embarrassing; some things are just between you and yourself, but to write is to tell someone to go long and hurl that part of yourself towards them. Frequently I'd curse God and die but then privately I'd say, 'I am so, so sorry, God, I'm so sorry.' Nobody ever puts away childish things because 1. There are so many of them, and 2. There isn't adequate storage space. The way, in front of friends, I might have said, 'Yeah, that toy cat is so stupid!' and tossed it down the stairs. Then later, alone, I'd cradle the toy cat in my arms and whisper, 'Please forgive me. Please. I'm so sorry.'

18

Chesterfield's Act of 1750 introduced the Gregorian calendar, already used by the majority of Europe, to Great Britain, losing us eleven days. In order for us to get into sync, 1751 was only 282 days long. Up to that point, the year began on March 25th, the Feast of the Annunciation. This is why, to this day, the tax year begins on April 6th, which, on the Old Style calendar, is March 25th. That's wild, right? So the darling buds of May are actually shaken by the rough winds, in the 16th century, during the month of June, i.e. Summer. I don't know if this is as important as it feels, but it feels important insofar as we might compare one another to a necessary adjustment which has unintended repercussions far beyond the administrative.

44

I would also like my skin to be thought, but it isn't. I have to carry it places, whereas thoughts have wings. A sub-party has started in the porch. We all have teleportation fantasies, but the quantum channel is always destroyed. So you could do it once and never come back. In such a way, in wishing it were otherwise, all science-fiction corresponds to our desire to renounce all responsibility for our actions. Crime fiction our desire to delegate. Criminality is bureaucracy in its purest uncut form. There is, though, some distant molecule forever altered, though you wouldn't know it, turning up on your doorstep like an unsolicited submission. A drastic, last-ditch signal. So you can go back once and try again but do exactly the same things differently and exactly the same things the same because you already went back. Teleport to the last ditch. The ribbons above the window say *Distraction is Perfidy*. If the dull substance of my thoughts were *skin* we'd walk along the skin-lined thoroughfare and pause under a fleshy, pulsating tree, I'd say, In all this hideous world you found me.

109

I had to urgently drive *three* cars a distance of approximately 12 miles. I forget the destination or the reason for the time pressure – someone was sick, someone was cold, there were children crying, we were in danger of missing something very important – but I felt it profoundly and for whatever reason I was the only one responsible for transport, perhaps the only one with a driving licence. It seemed to me at the time that *driving one car the entire 12 mile journey* and then *having to run 12 miles back to the remaining two cars*, then *drive the second car the complete journey* and then *having to run 12 miles back to the last car*, half dead with exhaustion, the taste of blood whenever I coughed, in order to *drive the third and final car the complete 12 miles*, having run and driven *a total of 60 miles* would be inefficient, if not impossible, both in terms of time and preserving my limited stamina. So I got in the first car and drove it as far as I could whilst I could still see the other two cars in the rear-view mirror (say about 2-300 metres? I'm between Metric and Imperial; kilometres mean *nothing* to me and neither do yards). I parked up the hill by a dry stone wall. I left it in a layby, the first car, ran back and collected the second car, drove it down the hill and parked it behind the first, then I ran back to retrieve the third car and parked it with the others, ready to begin the process again. Each time I was driving I was tempted to go farther, but I would drive the car as long a distance as possible so as not to feel like it was a waste of time having even started it, but as short a distance as possible so that running back to the other cars would be quick and not too difficult, the three chunky sets of keys clanking in my pocket as I ran, not entirely convinced that my plan was the best one but unable, which is not to say incapable, but yes, unable, to come up with an alternative.

North America Time, Poetry from the USA and Canada with Felicia McCarthy

Editorial

It is difficult
to get the news from poems
yet men die miserably every day
for lack
of what is found there.

—*William Carlos Williams*

It is not easy to keep writing poetry during this unprecedented time, but it is necessary. The poems coming in to North American Time from the USA and Canada are neither comfortable nor glorious. These poems are often nostalgic as writers look back, restless when reflecting chaos, and some simply drop into the present moment, most often into their own gardens and their own relationships- as you might expect during isolating months.

Poetry is changing, like the world itself. As the world copes with waves of pandemic rising and falling, as governments win and lose the battle of governance over an invisible foe, and a battle for the truth (some for and some against truth in news) all writers are writing their way into understanding the present moment.

If poetry is our world's Cassandra, if poets and writers often protest the wrongs, point to the right way forward, where do we find such poems now?

Here.

In every literary zine and zoom reading, every online collection of poets and pandemic poetry that manages to continue during the chaos, we find poets who keep writing to make sense of their own confusion, and by so doing help us find resonance with our own feelings.

I, like many poets here, turn back toward the ordinary as we process a fast changing world. All will be well, meanwhile we live in the hell of not knowing what is coming next, we must add the restrictions caused by chaos during the pandemic, and dare to write anyway.

As we read poetry now, we listen to differently nuanced voices, see from new perspectives.

We will be the better for waking up while staying tethered to the art of poetry where the real news is found as we write our way into the spaces made by the widening gyre. There is room for more voices than ever. The old *centre cannot hold*. We write to create a new more equitable core of a completely different society. Now is the time.

For this issue, we offer less but deliver more to keep The Blue Nib both affordable and relevant for us and for you. (Please do support us by subscription, if you are able.) Remember that The Blue Nib's digital platform continues to carry many voices that cannot be contained here, and has several poetry sections from the whole of the planet. www.thebluenib.com

At North American Time, I have five poets for you; three of these writers are well established, two are emerging poets. Among them are two emigrants to the USA, one very recently. Herein find one Japanese-American, Chinese-American, a recent emigrant from Romania, and two poets with a few generations of living as white Americans.

I will let you discover them for yourselves as you keep in mind the vast diversity in cultural heritage in these five poets. However, their themes- the challenge of a world pandemic, the difficulty of finding unity and relationship in a time of separation, and the great task of making peace in chaos- are yours, since human concerns are not restricted by any country's borders.

Felicia McCarthy
US/CAN Poetry Editor

Poetry by Mary Oishi

haiku in a pandemic

we must stay apart
now when we need each other
most, shelves bare of touch

***

when we can hug again
you're going to feel
a little bit warmer
I'm going to hold on
just a few seconds more

***

humans of the earth

you have the look of one
who crawled up out of the sea
took an IQ test
and invented fashion

Poetry by Carolyn Martin

In Praise of Community
– with thanks to Merriam-Webster Online

A coterie of chick-a-dees
communes
in my maple tree.
A tribe of constellations
self-distances
in a nightfall sky.
Brown-robed monastics
bow
before breaking bread.
Circles of poets
zoom
from their living rooms.
Fellowships of love
connect
black/brown/yellow/white/red.

Let's praise
every synonym
that binds, bonds, ties, unites
and make a communal vow:
if any family, circle,
troop, guild, league,
club, or neighborhood
morphs
into a clique, sect, gang,
faction, or closed shop,
we'll revise
our acclaim and delete
our membership
without
a moment's doubt.

Pay attention and you're saved.

It pays to pay attention – which is not
like paying bills, the pizza delivery guy,
or the piper – wherever he may pipe.
Nor is it like paying compliments,
taxes, penalties, dues, visits, respect,
or up-down-forward-back for anything.

Crime doesn't pay, unless it does.
Neither does arrogance when you nip
your own line to title this poem.

But when oblivion's about to hit
pay dirt and saving's worth a fight,
rouse attention, slumped in the doorway

of your shuttered mind. Focus its eyes
on barefaced possibilities peeking
through blossoms of an aging cherry tree.

Poetry by Adina Dabija

The Garden's Invitation

I did want to belong
to a place, or a time, or at least to a man
but I had to learn non locality
I had to learn to build the garden anywhere
from the quicksilver of a dew drop
rolling on a leaf that existed only in my imagination
somewhere in Alhambra
where water and stone flow into each other
just like spirit flows into matter

And when I got confined to small apartments
of crowded cities with eye of the needle size spaces
I was shown to sow seeds
of roses, and mints and petunias
that grow lush up to the sky
with birds and butterflies
expanding
breathing
reminding me of something so rarefied
that can only be expressed as scent or wings flutter
Let me dwell in that language!

And when amidst struggles,
when life pulled me in all directions,
the gardener herself called me in the garden
to show me how to make
rows and spirals moving with the stars
order and harmony
orchestrated by the loving touch of an invisible hand
like in Konya's garden
where roses sway in the wind whispering love's name

Century after century,
season after season,
the garden has always kept its gates open
- take a walk!
part of you needs to overflow here
in this sunlight.

Crescent Moon

The crescent moon shines its sharp blade
on your forties
you are at your midlife

you are ripe like peaches in July
ready to be sacrificed
split in two
offered to the invisible

one half will stay on earth
the other one will be offered up
just like the moon offers herself to the sunlight

This is your first death
it's a good one
take it!

Poetry by Jeff Santosuosso

Swan

From a board, a platform, or a ledge,
step carefully. Deliberate. Lift off.
Leap to the bottoms of the clouds.
Reach your fingers toward the sky.

Step carefully, deliberate, lift off
your cares and trepidations.
Reach your fingers toward the sky.
Point your toes to the bottom of the sea.

Your cares and trepidations
release off the wingtips of your arms.
Point your toes to the bottom of the sea
to slice the water as thin as water itself.

Release the wingtips of your arms.
Open yourself to the sky
to slice the water as thin as water itself.
Bare yourself to the sea, to nature.

Open yourself to the sky.
Reach out, touch down.
Bare yourself to the sea, to nature
as you descend, muscular, rippling.

Reach out, touch down
taut fibers connecting sky and sea
as you descend, muscular, rippling
to what informs you as subject, object.
Bare yourself to the sea, to nature.

I Am Here

Men jump from the sky
Men shoot toddlers dead
Men rape their sisters
work three jobs, sleep three hours
I am here.

Men stand in the rain,
run from the hail
scorch the land with fire and chemicals
I am here.

My circle has shrunk
so few intersections
It's all news, not even paper
far-off reports in a far-out medium
where my life no longer goes
I am here.

I see the moon, I see the horizon
I feel the sun warm the sky.
There are there, aren't they?
I am here.

What black hole beams this way
what comet tail trails my heavens
what lava flows, burns, cools, becomes rock,
a black, sharp path where once was footfall
I am here.

Winds beckon the dawn of life,
emissaries from ages ago
this strange circling forth
we call it hurricane, tornado
minutes, hours, days long, then normalized
I am here.

Poetry by Pui Ying Wong

BLUING

The sky is blue, and bullets fly.

The sky is blue, and bullets fly.

The sky is blue, and bullets fly.

The sky is blue, and bullets fly.

Along a wild river and old villages,

Hung laundry and rubble,

Summer camp and freshwater, bullets fly.

The sky is blue, the sky is blue, the sky is blue.

In classrooms and in cinemas, in cafes

And in churches, in shopping malls and discos,

In barracks with flower beds and greenway, bullets fly,

Bullets fly, bullets fly, bullets fly.

In Sunday school amid bowed heads

And sacred texts, in parking lots

And on streets and highways, bullets fly.

Today, a man, a woman opens the door

To a blue sky, too blue,

The sky is blue.

The sky is blue.

The sky is blue.

The sky is blue.

OF THE EARTH

Leave the window, let the bed

receive you like a simple lover.

Hear the small wind that tugs

at the curtain, the universe's soft arc.

Let childhood's lunar moon return, how

it trails after you like a loyal friend.

For so long you've gone from

here to there,

    sometimes alone,

with others like a flotilla of stars.

You've learned one truth, you are worthy

of the earth's bitter roots. Sleep.

It's okay no one knows your sorrow

just as they don't know your joy.

Night still arrives for you, in splendor,

familiar as you own breath.

SUNSET OVER AMHERST

An empty gazebo.

After dinner.

The sky turns,

kinks

of the day

smoothed.

Few paths converged

here,

one to the lake,

the other to the road,

one more to our studio.

Uneven patches of grass,

unknown berries,

ivies wild

around the bend.

The moon has a chip.

Pen scratches on paper.

Michael Morpurgo in conversation with Clare Morris

Michael Morpurgo (Sir Michael Andrew Bridge Morpurgo, OBE, FRSL, FKC) is an immensely popular and much-loved author, poet and playwright, although he prefers the term 'story-maker'. Perhaps best-known for 'War Horse', a story which tells of the experiences of Joey, a horse sold to the army in the First World War, Michael Morpurgo has published well over 100 books. He is passionate about the importance of literature as a means of helping you to 'look beyond yourself'.

He and his wife, Clare, established the charity 'Farms For City Children' in 1976, with the aim of providing children from inner-city areas with experience of the countryside. The charity now has three farms. To date, 100,000 children have appreciated the benefits of living close to nature by staying on these farms.

I met him in the garden of The Duke of York pub in Iddesleigh, Devon, not far from his home. We spoke for over an hour. He wanted to hear, first of all, about our work at The Blue Nib. The interview below starts as I conclude my explanation and we begin to talk about 'War Horse'.

In our wide-ranging discussion, we explore his books, his craft, his early experiences, his friendships, his belief in the value of children's literature, his charity work and his hopes for the future. I have included subheadings in this interview to direct you to key areas of our conversation.

My interview with Michael Morpurgo was a rare, unexpected gift, for which I am immensely grateful. I am sure you will be too.

Clare Morris
Editor of The Write life

The challenge: 'to get people reading from a very young age'

MM: So the idea is to keep it going?
CM: Yes, it looks as if we can get back on track with publishing four magazines a year.
MM: And it's an important year for that too so you can take a deep breath and continue planning. Well that's the challenge of it, that's for sure, to get people reading from a very young age. All power to you. I think it's lovely to find other people batting on the same wicket as I'm on. You don't realise until you meet them, so it's very nice.
CM: Thank you because it's obviously very close to our hearts to create a platform for emerging writers.
MM: So, you're in Devon, aren't you? Do you know this pub?
CM: Well, I was going to ask about that. It was going to be my first question.
MM: Well, fire away. We've got about forty minutes. Is that alright?
CM: Yes, that's wonderful.

'War Horse': 'stories grow up on stories'

CM: We're at 'The Duke of York', with its links with 'War Horse'. Is there more to your association with the place than that?
MM: Well it's interesting really because as with all these things, as you know, stories grow up on stories. They come out of nowhere and the original reason that we're here is unbelievably literary, which might appeal to your readers. My wife is called Clare and her daddy was a publisher, a great publisher, probably the greatest of the 20th century, Allen Lane, who started Penguin books. He knew the lady (this is bizarre) who ran this pub in the 1940s, just after the Second World War. He was up in London, doing what he was doing with his publishing and she was running the Windmill nightclub. She was the Publicity Director. She was called Peggy Rafferty and she and Allen Lane were good friends, how good we don't know, but good friends and just after the war was over, Peggy Rafferty decided to come down to Devon and buy this pub with her new husband, a man called Seán Rafferty, who was a considerable poet, someone who might be known in literary magazines. Seán and Peggy ran this pub for 25 years or more, worked hard, got in the Good Food Guide. He was behind the bar and hated every moment, I think, but she loved it. Anyway, way before that, Allen Lane had this daughter called Clare who I think was a bit of a pain in the neck and needed occupying during the school holidays so he said to Peggy, 'Can I bring Clare down to look at the place with a view possibly to her coming and having holidays with you, on her own? Because she's an independent little girl.' And Clare loved it. Her little room's up there (*he points across the garden to a window on the second floor*) and looks out across the way. So, she had a room there and came back every holiday between the age of about 7 and 12. This was her home and she got to know all the people round and about on

her walks about the place and loved it to bits. Peggy looked after her as best she could but in a sense, in the nicest possible way, wanted her to be out, during the day, walking and walking and walking, not hanging around the pub and getting under the feet of the guests. So, that's what she did; she'd put on her wellies and off she'd go. She was the one who discovered this place and her love for it, which years and years later made us come here to start 'Farms for City Children' which is our project. Our whole reason for starting up was because she had had this extraordinary experience here: a little girl growing up here and finding out about not just farms but about nature and little creepy crawly things. She was a suburban girl. It was all strange to her. People were friendly, and would give her lemonade and sticky buns and she'd groom the horses and feed the calves and she became this wandering child in the days when you could do this in the 40s and 50s. So, then we thought of setting up, as teachers, 'Farms for City Children' because we thought children needed more than a classroom – the countryside is a wonderful classroom, use it. Her daddy died in 1970 sadly and when he died, he left us some money. So, she thought she'd put the money where her mouth had been and bought a big house, Nethercott House, about a mile outside the village here and invited schools from the Inner London Education Authority and they started coming and coming. That was 45 years ago and we've got 3 farms now and 100,000 children have been so that's the story behind this place although I know it's known for 'War Horse' now.

We moved down here in 1976 and were strangers. The people who ran the pub knew Clare very well so introduced us to everyone. I'd come along to the pub as you do and meet people. I happened to meet, by pure accident, one of the three men I was told had been to the First World War, who were then octogenarians and they lived in the village still. One of them I found sitting by the fire, a bloke called Wilf Ellis. I knew who he was and a bit about his story, that he'd been to the First World War, so I started asking him about it and he said, 'I was there with the horses.' He started talking about being there and the things that happened to him as a 17 year old boy and the fact that the horse was his best friend without question because he could say things to this horse that he could never say to his friends about fear, about longing and all these things. So, the whole idea of a relationship between a young soldier and a horse started there and of course there was a sale in 1914 on the village green of local farm horses to the army.

So much that was part of the history of this place I used in the story, which is what I do anyway. That's how I do writing. I'm not brilliant at fantasy, I tend to grow stories out of history or memory or other people's stories. Never, if you like, out of the nothingness. You need a proper imagination for that like Philip Pullman's got or Lewis Carroll or someone like that. Anyway, this pub has become a little bit associated with 'War Horse' but it has a much longer history as far as we're concerned. And we still live here; we're not going to go anywhere else now. Actually, it's very strange that in the pandemic it's one of the safest places in the world you can be. So, we're very lucky.

'War Horse': 'the seed corn for building confidence'

CM: Did you realise, when you wrote 'War Horse', that it would be so successful?
MM: No, well, at the time, I'd never had any success at writing; I'd just finished books, that's all the success that I thought was possible. I earned a few pounds from it but never very much, I had one or two things that were reprinted, most that weren't. I had one or two really interesting, small things which were the seed corn for building confidence because writing is so much about confidence. Without that you really can't even finish the first page. I wrote one or two little stories for an education series for Macmillan, when I was a teacher. Very often writers begin that way. You write for the children you teach, which I did. I tried out my story telling with them. I grew in the classroom when I was teaching. Before we came to live here and started the project, while we were in Kent, I taught for about eight years at the coal face and they never learned any Mathematics or anything like that, they just learned to write. We spent a lot of time reading other people's things, poetry. I remember particularly a book by Ted Hughes called 'Poetry In The Making'. I tried to encourage them to find their voices, their own confidence, that they had something to say and following what Ted had said, you look and you listen and you feel and you keep yourself open and vulnerable. That's the way you drink in the world and then you've got something to write about.
And what did we find when we got down here? Ted Hughes lived about five miles away from here. He became the President for 'Farms for City Children' and I got to know him through that. By the time 'War Horse' came along, we'd got to know him quite well.
But going back to the whole business of did one know – no, not a clue. I was hopeful but one or two people said, 'Yes but it's sort of like 'Black Beauty' isn't it?' And I said, 'Well in one sense it is, the horse tells the story but that doesn't matter. There are lots of books written by writers where the writer tells the story and it's alright to do what they do, so I can write one as if a horse has written it.'

'War Horse': 'so I decided, let that horse speak the story'

I did get the idea for that, no, not the idea, the *confidence* to be able to do that, because it is a pretty silly thing to do. Here was I trying to set out to write a story about the First World War and the whole purpose of my writing the story was *not* to write another war book. There are many, many books about war and almost always they are written from one side or the other. My idea was to try to write a story, if possible, from all sides so that it was a story of the universal suffering of the First World War. So, I decided then that you needed a neutral observer and because of this conversation I'd had with Wilf Ellis, I thought OK, we'll let the horse be the neutral observer. All sides had horses; they all used horses, so I decided, let that horse speak the story and be the neutral eye.
I was very frightened at the beginning because it was a risk. You can be ridiculous if

you're not careful, doing this sort of thing. It could have been very sentimental but to get away from that, I had to be convinced myself that it *wasn't* sentimental. I had a little incident which happened where the children come at Nethercott *(Nethercott House, one of the Farms for City Children),* just down the road. There was a little kid from Birmingham who had had major problems with speaking. There had been some trauma and he didn't speak all week. The teacher said, 'Well, he just doesn't speak. He's been with us at school, he never speaks. Don't ask him questions, Michael, because he might run back to Birmingham because he gets very frightened if he's made to try to speak – and then it shows other people that he can't or won't. Don't make him.' So I was as tactful as I could be and I noticed he never said a word all week, not to the teachers, not to his pals. He had pals but they were all silent pals really. They treated him, I think, as if he was dumb and deaf. There was nothing nasty about it, that's how they took it.

'War Horse': 'that horse valued the trust that this boy was giving'

I came in one night to read them a story, Thursday night, the night before they went home, a dark November night, cold, and I walked into the stable yard behind this big Victorian house and there was a horse leaning out of the stable, Hebe she was called, and this boy was there, Billy. He was in his dressing gown and his slippers and it was raining so I was about to say to him, 'Billy, go inside' and then, before I had a chance to speak, I realised he was talking – and he was talking to the horse. So he was standing under the head of the horse, if you can imagine it, with his hand up on the side of the horse's face, just resting there, not patting, just resting, and talking, talking, talking, talking, nineteen to the dozen, there wasn't a hesitation. So, I thought the teachers have to see this. So I went and fetched the teachers. We all crept round through the vegetable garden and we stayed hidden in the garden and we listened to this boy talking to this horse about all the things he'd done that day, just flowing and flowing and flowing. Then I noticed something which was even more important than that and that was, and this is where a lot of people leave me and don't believe it, and that was that the horse was listening. And I sensed, and I'm sure I was absolutely right, that that horse valued the trust that this boy was giving, the affection, the love, whatever you want to call it, and stayed there and listened and of course didn't understand a word but understood what was going on in the boy's heart. And it was important. They had created a relationship together.
 I'd often heard my wife, Clare, and others, when they were with the horses in the stables, talking to the horses and, to start with, I remember thinking, that's stupid, you know, but actually that calms the horse, that's part of the person that you are. Anyway, that's why I wrote it but I didn't expect, to answer your question properly, anything to happen except the book would come out. It nearly won a prize, was shortlisted for the Whitbread Prize and didn't win it. Some other beggar won it.

'War Horse': 'it's not a children's book because children don't like history' (Roald Dahl)

It's funny, I don't know if you know this but among the people who were judging it was a man called Roald Dahl, you might have heard of him. Well, Roald Dahl was the chair and after it was all over at this dinner, on telly it was, I was called up by him, the finger beckoned like this (*he crooks his finger*). Well, he was the Great Master - not as far as I was concerned, I mean I rated him but I didn't rate him that highly. He called me up and said, 'Well it's a good book, a very good book, but it's not a children's book because children don't like history.' I said, 'OK, well, there we are.' The Master had spoken and of course, it's completely wrong. It depends how you tell the story, that's the truth of it. But anyway, there you go, it didn't win. But in a way that was a blessing because to win a prize quite young is not necessarily a good idea. It was a disappointment and the book sat there for 25 years. It never sold more than a couple of thousand a year maximum.

The hardback, I have to tell you this because it's a lovely story – the hardback had a wonderful cover by a great illustrator called Victor Ambrus, he was Hungarian but lived here all his life. He was also responsible for Henry Treece's illustrations for Puffin – he does history terribly well and he did a beautiful cover for 'War Horse', the best cover, I think, that's ever been, in the first edition in hardback. If you go into a rare bookshop now, you'll find it, if you're lucky, you'll find it for sale, but it's extraordinarily rare , not because the book is totally brilliant but because so few copies were printed and so few people bought them. The current value of a first edition of 'War Horse' is £1,500 … which is twice as much as I got paid for writing the entire book. So, it's quite fun. I love all these things.

'War Horse' on stage and screen: 'a big light shone on it'

Anyway, the reason of course it shot to fame 25 years later was the National Theatre; it wasn't Spielberg, it was the National Theatre and a wonderful man called Tom Morris. He was looking for a way of using some amazing puppeteers. Anyway, at the centre of this play are these puppets, huge life size puppets, designed by Handspring Puppets from South Africa. Tom Morris was a director there and wanted to use these people for a major play. Puppets as you know tend to be peripheral, accompanying the main actors. So, he was looking for a story that had an animal at its heart but centre stage and his mother heard me speaking on 'Desert Island Discs', wittering on about 'War Horse' a bit and thought it was interesting. She happened to be in an Oxfam bookshop a few days later and saw an old paperback copy of 'War Horse', picked it up, read it, thought it was good, rang up her son and said, 'You know you were looking for a horse story or an animal story, try 'War Horse''. So, he did what his mother said.

Then of course it became flavour of the month for a bit and then Spielberg came along, saw the play because his producer was in London by accident with a horsey daughter who wanted to see the play. They went in, liked it, she rang up Spielberg, he came over a week later and within a year you have a film – that only happens with Spielberg, it's just extraordinary. And, of course, because of that it was suddenly a best seller in New York, it was a best seller in London and here's this book which had been sitting around for 25 years, no one even looking at it – it's very funny. It just shows you what the whole thing is down to: it's good fortune to get published and it's good fortune if a book gets noticed. You can only do so much with publicity. Someone's got to pick it up and run with it. Reviews help, of course they do, but it's not the same thing as a big light shone on it. A play can do that, a film can do that and I'm very, very grateful to both Tom Morris and Steven Spielberg because of course the book is now widely read, translated into, I don't know what it is, 50 languages. In a way you get known as 'The War Horse author' and I don't mind that. It's really lovely that there's one book at least, which has leapt up and away from the others. I'd far rather it was known for something rather than for nothing and it helps the other books. It all helps the other books to get published.

Early influences: 'poems that were visceral in some way'

CM: I was going to ask about 'Private Peaceful' as well.
MM: Of course, it's set in this village.
CM: Yes, teachers, in their teaching schemes, will progress from 'War Horse' to 'Private Peaceful.' I wonder, when you were writing 'Private Peaceful', did you have the idea that that's what teachers would do or did you see the books as stand-alones?
MM: Oh, complete stand-alones. I mean, I was interested of course because of 'War Horse' in the First World War but I was interested before that. Again, it's interesting with your questions because they go back further than that, and the reason I'm interested, I suppose, in the subject of conflict is because when I grew up as a teenager, the first poems I ever liked were the War Poets. There was Owen, there was Sassoon, there was Edward Thomas. They were the first poems that meant something. I didn't really like poems about daffodils, aged 16. They really didn't do it for me, do you know what I mean? But poems that were visceral in some way, about the human condition, however dark it might be, I thought, 'I can identify with that.'
I went into the army for a bit, for a year, so I had a glimpse of what it was to be a soldier, the camaraderie and also what might happen if you get out there and do it for real. I left pretty quick and went into teaching, marginally less dangerous, and in a way, I wouldn't say I was conditioned but I certainly was prepared for that meeting that I had with Wilf Ellis in the pub and there, of course, I was speaking for the first time in my life to a real veteran and not just someone who'd interpreted it for a play or a film or anything else. That was an extraordinary moment.

'I'm sure it's the same for every writer, you just come across stuff'

With 'Private Peaceful', because I'd already had this dip into the history of the First World War and the conditions of the people who lived with it, I went to Ypres in Belgium. I'm sure it's the same for every writer, you just come across stuff, like I came across Wilf Ellis in the pub. When I was in Ypres, I went to the museum. There's a museum there called 'In Flanders Fields', which is about the best interpretive exhibition of war that I know. I came out of the museum very moved by everything I'd seen and heard. It's the war from all sides; it's not about the British or the Belgians or the French or the Americans – it's about all of us who were involved in that horror. In that sense, that's one of the things I really liked about it. It wasn't like going to the Imperial War Museum which is so much about us. This is about the whole thing.

Private Peaceful 'the tear is what made me write the book'

As I was coming out, I saw this frame on the wall and there was a scrappy looking piece of paper in it and an envelope and I just happened to glance at it. It was a letter, written, well, *typed* by an officer, a lieutenant, to a mother, a Mrs Someone, didn't know who, and on the envelope there was the name and the address. The letter said, 'We regret to inform you that your son, Private So and So and the number, was shot at dawn for cowardice on such and such a date.' Signed, that's it. Then there was this envelope which had been opened out so that you could see the tear and the tear is what made me write the book because I just thought, hang on, this woman had stood on her doorstep, I think it was in somewhere like Salford, and she'd opened the envelope with a bit of a tear and what was in that envelope was to destroy her life and the life of her family. I thought this is just extraordinary. I felt very passionately that to shoot a man for that sort of thing was just awful and I went to the man who ran the museum, a man called Piet Chielens who's a great authority on the First World War, and I said , 'Do you have, by any chance, anywhere I could read a trial of these people?' And he said, 'Yes, I've got twenty of them downstairs.' So I went and looked and I read the trials of these soldiers. There were over 300 shot for cowardice or desertion. Two because they fell asleep while on guard. I thought to myself I must read those so I took three or four of the photocopies back to the hotel. I read them that night. I read three out of the four. When I read them, I realised they were less than half an hour long … for a man's life. You could tell when the people started with the questions that they'd already made up their mind. Far too many of them were Irish or Black and you realised there was an agenda here. Also, you could see the spikes; just before an offensive, these trials were taken much, much more seriously and there were more people condemned and of course it was to encourage other soldiers not to do the same thing. Anyway, I thought, let's take one of these people, I didn't know who. I didn't take one of those cases.

'what an extraordinary name'

I just took one soldier, I grew him up here in the village of Iddesleigh. He's a farm worker's son, his family lives near to the village, where I live in my cottage. They ring the bells here in the church, that's the whole sort of place he grew up in and he and his brother love the same girl, it happens, and they went off to war together. It's the story of these brothers and they're called Peaceful because of a graveyard outside Ypres. It's called the Bedford Cemetery, which is, I think, 5 miles outside. My wife and I were walking, which we do from time to time. In fact, we make it rather a religious thing; when we go there, which we've done a lot, we don't just go and have a nice Belgian meal, we tend to go to one of the graveyards. This one we were just driving past, so we said, 'Let's go to this one.' There were about 3000 graves there, I think. We were just walking along in the graveyard and my wife said, 'Look, what an extraordinary name, Private Peaceful.' So, we went to Piet Chielens and I said, 'Do you know anything about this Private Peaceful, who had died, 26, I think?' He looked him up, no family enquiries, nothing like that, so I said, 'In that case, I suppose it's probably alright to borrow the name, isn't it?' So I did.
Then shortly after the book was published, I got a letter from someone called Peaceful. I think they live in Southampton. He was a relative of theirs. They didn't mind at all, they were fine about it but then a remarkable thing happened, truly remarkable. They discovered that the name on the grave had been spelt wrong. The real soldier had two ls. My soldier, who's now a fiction, had one. And what did they do? What are they called, the organisation that looks after graves?

CM: The Commonwealth War Graves Commission.
MM: The War Graves Commission. So last year, we went over and had a ceremony where they replaced the gravestone with his proper name which would not have happened without the book.

'Private Peaceful': 'when the world changes, it'll be through education'

There's another thing that doesn't happen without the book. I know when the world changes it'll be through education, nothing else.....what's really wonderful is that many, many schools have picked up on that book. As you say, it's read in Secondary schools quite a lot and they make a trip specially out there on coaches from all over England and that's one of the places where they visit, Private Peaceful's grave. I was doing something for the BBC, 3 or 4 years after 'Private Peaceful' came out. It had attracted a bit of attention and so they wanted an interview. I did a radio interview in another graveyard, not the same one, and I was standing there with a sound recordist and someone else with a camera and this coach turned up. A huge coach and it said Epsom on the outside. Then about 50 kids, teenagers, 15 years old, poured out, making quite a noise, so we had to stop recording. I got a bit cross because as they came into this graveyard, they were making a lot of noise and I thought the teacher

should have quietened them down, calmed them down and I was about to say something when an extraordinary thing happened: they did calm down and quieten down but it was because of the place.
They all walked off in twos and threes, no one was giggling, no one was laughing. They were just walking around and the teacher noticed me because I was wearing a red jacket, which I wear sometimes, and said, 'Are you the person that wrote 'Private Peaceful'?' and I said, 'Yes, well, that's the reason we're here. But he's not buried here.' She said, 'I know, we've just come from Bedford Cemetery. We've made Private Peaceful our Unknown Soldier and read the book because it's important.' The teacher was really enlightened. She said, 'There's no point in reading about the millions and the millions. That's not interesting. What's interesting is one soldier. Because we've read this book, it's one story, we know it's fiction based on the experience of so many, Private Peaceful is our Unknown Soldier. So when we came here, we found his grave and back at school we had made a wreath and we'd written letters. It was drizzling a bit so we've wrapped it all in cellophane and you can go there and see it.' And so I did. I went there and saw it and it was extraordinary. These people had been there and they'd left their letters that they'd written to Private Peaceful. It was lovely; so, in a sense you could see the consequences of writing a book like that which is a great privilege for a writer: to be able to physically see it.

Music: 'I've no idea why music seems to get through to people in the way it does. But it does.'

CM: Could I ask about the ending of 'Private Peaceful'? The use of 'Oranges and Lemons' – it's so defiant and haunting. Whenever I hear the tune now, it just brings me back to the book.
MM: Oh, it's ruined that particular children's song for you.
CM: No, no, it hasn't; it's imbued it with something else. I'm just wondering about the importance of music in your work.
MM: Ah it's huge, really huge.
CM: What does it give you?
MM: I liked singing when I was little. I played the violin extremely badly but I did like singing in the choir. I went to a very musical school in Canterbury, a place called The King's School, Canterbury. The music was just extraordinary, so I was immersed really in music, and at home as well. I fell in love with Mozart at a very early age. Yes, music does imbue the stories and I do a lot of concerts now. There's a book I wrote called 'The Mozart Question' – do you know the book?
CM: Yes
MM: We do a concert with a group, a quartet, and we play the music that might have been played – and was played - in the concentration camps. There is an enormous power in music.
It's interesting, just at the moment, how music and stories have meant a great deal

more in this lockdown than they've ever meant before. I think everyone's sick of series on television because it flows over your head, but there's something about music which is immersive, and it touches places. I've no idea why music seems to get through to people in the way it does. But it does. Its power is amazing. I hope words can do it sometimes and certainly the association of words and music.

Music: 'that's what I love, when music and words come together in tone and in power'

Funnily enough, I'll tell you something I'm doing just now, literally now, oh this is a… what do you call it?... a *scoop*. I don't think anyone else knows about this. I'm going off on Sunday to do a recording at that studio in London, you know where the Beatles did their stuff, the Abbey Road Studios. I'm doing it for Decca and I'm doing it with an extraordinary group of players, all of whom are from one family. He's called Sheku Kanneh-Mason and his entire family. They are going to be playing 'Carnival of the Animals'.
CM: Saint-Saëns.
MM: And they asked me to write 14 poems to go in between the pieces for this recording we're going to make. So, I did that and they seemed to like it. They also, because it's a CD and it has to be a little bit longer, chose a book of mine called 'Grandpa Christmas'. This group, all kids, these amazing people, the Magnificent Musical Seven, I think of them as, they chose music to weave through 'Grandpa Christmas' which they're going to play. I'm going to read that and Olivia Coleman is going to read the poems with me in the first part. So, in a way, to answer your question, that's what I love, when music and words come together in tone and in power, which is what I hope we've done. And I think they're going to finish it bizarrely, wonderfully bizarrely actually, with their own arrangement of 'Redemption Song' by Bob Marley. It's one of those CDs which is going to be out for Christmas. Anyway, *you* know.
CM: Thank you!
MM: I didn't tell The Daily Mail first!

Early Development: 'I'm a story-maker'

CM: Could we backtrack to your own development as a writer, early on. When did you first realise that you were a writer?
MM: I never did really. I still don't. I'm a story-maker. I'm quite spontaneous about it really and I don't necessarily like the words 'author' or 'writer' because actually what we all are from Shakespeare to Bob Dylan, we are all story makers. We tell different stories and we tell them in a different way and that's, finally, what we are. So, I make stories, I tell tales.
I got into it because my mum used to read me stories when I was very little, which I loved. I hated books at school because they made you do comprehension and they

made you have spelling tests and they made you have punctuation tests – I walked away from literature until I was well out of my teens. I read only what I had to read for O level and A level, played rugby and that sort of thing. It was only when I found myself in front of a class of children and telling stories, not reading, just telling stories that I heard or wanted to tell, that I suddenly found there was an enormous power in this, which is the same power that my mother had when she was reading to me and I remembered it. To be fair, I'd had one or two teachers through my school years who had also had this same power and particularly at university. I remember at university, there was one teacher called Garmonsway. This was at Kings College, London. He was teaching us 'Beowulf' and he would sit on the corner of his desk, in his tweedy old suit and puff his pipe, and just read it. He read it like my mother read it, with enormous conviction and passion, not like a teacher. He was telling us the story because he loved it and that's what came across with my mother. That's what I'd do with the children in my Year 6 class at Wickhambreaux Primary School. I told stories either from the page or ones that I'd made up but I told them with complete conviction. I told them as if it was true and made it true for them and I loved doing that. It gave me more and more confidence when I was telling them.

Writing: 'it's a matter of confidence and habit'

I had a wonderful headteacher called Mrs Skiffington who came in to listen to me one day because she'd heard about my storytelling, in the playground I think or it had been reported to her; so she came and sat at the back. Afterwards she said, 'That was really good, Michael. You should write it out and give it to me on Monday morning.' So I did. I wrote it out and gave it to her on Monday morning. She knew someone who worked at Macmillan and said, 'You should send the story off.' I sent the story off and I got a reply. They said, 'We really like your story. Would you write 5 more and we'll pay you, I remember, £75.' So, I thought, eat your heart out, Roald Dahl. Anyway, that's how I got started.
Honestly, it's a matter of confidence and habit. This lockdown's been very interesting. What am I now, 77, and I've never written so much, so hard or so intensely in all my life. Well, most of the time it's because there's no option. I've been in my little bubble down the road, not seeing anyone for five months and I wrote and I wrote and I wrote. So, I've retold the tales of Shakespeare, as Lamb did, all those years ago, in my own way. I've written lots of poetry and short stories. It becomes what I do every day and, without it, I feel rather wretched.
CM: So what's your typical writing day like? Is there one?
MM: I can actually tell you. There's no typical writing day but I can tell you what's happened during lockdown. I do all my writing in the morning, I don't get dressed, I don't shave, I just have a bit of breakfast and then I just go and sit in my bed, which is where I scribble and write until about half past twelve. Then I might get up, not necessarily, take my jimjams off and get dressed, make myself a little bit respectable, have lunch. Then, in the afternoon, it's rest time for a couple of hours,

then a walk down to the river, Tarka's river by the way, the River Torridge, where so many great poets like Ted Hughes and Seamus Heaney and others have walked. I think a lot about that when I'm down there, do a lot of thinking, then I watch a film in the evening or something like that – and that's my day. It's been very, very, very regular, not going out at all, of course. Everyone's brought us everything because we're the oldest people in the lane and people have been so kind, really, really lovely; so much so we're feeling rather spoilt and we're finding it rather difficult to climb back into the real world, which we've got to do. But that's my routine and generally speaking, that's how it should be.

My slight problem is that if you do bring out books, there's a kind of a compulsion that you should go out and market them, for festivals and schools and stuff like that, which normally I quite like doing but I do live miles away from everyone and it's a long, long way to go places. I've travelled this country for the last 20 years up and down, up and down, sometimes to no effect at all. Sometimes it's lovely but it's up and down. It's very hit and miss, these festivals and school visits. I'll do less now, there's no question of it, because I did find it very exhausting. My wife finds it exhausting too because she comes with me if she possibly can and she prefers to be home. That's one thing we've learned, we both prefer to be home. I think the routines will change. I'll do more sitting here and going for walks. That sort of thing.

'War Horse': 'I've had time to think it through and it's got a better ending'

CM: You've got some books coming out in the Autumn, haven't you? Could you tell us about those?

MM: Ah yes, there's one interesting thing. It's probably just the publishers squeezing the juice out of something but they felt, and I think it's true, that it would be quite nice to have a 'War Horse' adaptation for younger children. So, it's a huge illustrated book and done in the kind of illustrations they would like. It's a simplified story, changed a bit, improved actually; it's the best version of the story because I've had time to think it though and it's got a better ending, I think. Anyway, so that's coming out. It's just called 'War Horse', published by Egmont Books.

CM: That's a teaser, better ending.

MM: Better ending. It's taken a long time, it's taken a really long time to get a better ending, hasn't it, really? With the play, the ending is OK, with the film, well, I'll say nothing about the ending but this particular one, it's the best. Then there's a book called 'Owl or Pussycat', published by David Fickling Books. It occurred to me that when you first go to Primary School, whatever happens at that school for all children, it's the first time. Everything is a first at a Primary School and for me it was the first time I fell in love, aged 6. I never really told the story but it was also the first time that I was ever in a play. The school put on a play every Christmas time and this year it was going to be 'The Owl and the Pussycat.' I got lucky. Because my mother read to me such a lot, she read me poems as well. She had read me 'The

Owl and the Pussycat' and it happened to be my favourite poem and so I knew it by heart. When the teacher read it to the whole class, she said afterwards, 'Do any of you know that poem?' I said, 'I know it by heart.' And so she said, 'Do you, Michael. Could you stand up and say it then?'

So I did, and she was so pleased that, when it came to casting the play, I was Owl and here's the thing: the girl who was chosen to play the Pussycat was this girl I was in love with. I hadn't told her that, but I was. So, we did the play and I'm not going to tell you what happened. It was a disaster. Naturally. And we didn't make it up, it really was a disaster… and to have a disaster in front of 200 people…But the interesting thing is that I've been back to the school. It's called St Cuthbert's with St Mathias and it's on the Warwick Road in London. Still there, still the same building, still the same parquet floor which is in the story. So I dedicated it to the children and they come down to the farm now. The kids from the school now come down to the farm. So, we've made a sort of relationship there. I'm going to launch it in the very hall in which the play was performed, let's get this right, in 1950. So, that's coming out with wonderful illustrations.

New Titles: 'more exciting really is the connection to the story I first told you'

In a way, just as exciting, but more exciting really, is the connection to the story I first told you. My main publisher is HarperCollins and I haven't got a book coming out with them, I've got some paperback things but I haven't got a new book coming out. The story is that I was approached by Puffin Books, because it's going to be the 80th anniversary of the founding of Puffin Books and of course the person who founded Puffin Books is my father-in-law, Allen Lane. That is why they approached me and said, 'Would you do something to celebrate? Would you write a story? Maybe about a puffin.' So I couldn't refuse, the wife would have been a bit upset. I was very flattered to be asked and I'd done one or two things for them before anyway. So, I thought, yes, and I've written the story. It's called 'The Puffin Keeper' and it's about the Isles of Scilly and a lighthouse and an old man who keeps the lighthouse and rescues some people from a ship coming in from America, a great four-masted schooner, all those years and years ago. He rescues people and brings them back to his island, to his lighthouse and one of them is a small boy. It's the story of the relationship between this old lighthouse keeper and this boy. After he's been rescued, they pick him up the next day and the others that have been rescued, his mother included. The lighthouse keeper has noticed that this little boy has spent quite a lot of time looking at all the pictures on the wall of the lighthouse, which he's painted. Every single one is of a boat, a ship. It's in the style of a naïve artist from St Ives, it's modelled on him. Anyway, the boy's got his eye on one painting and the old man notices this. It's a tiny painting, and he gives it to him. It's all done on wood. The boy takes it and it becomes a sort of talisman; he keeps it all the way through his life. So, we follow this boy through his life until he's a man. I try to link it back to the main story because Allen Lane had two brothers who he founded

Penguin Books with, one of whom was called John. I think he was his favourite brother. John was killed in the Second World War. He went down in an aircraft carrier in the Mediterranean, when it was torpedoed so there is someone in the book who is called John Lane and he does go down. He's a friend of this young boy when he grows up and joins the Navy. The boy finally comes back to see this old man and it's all really about what this old man has done with his life, what the boy has done with his life, who is now a man, and how … I won't tell you that or you won't buy the book. Anyway, I'm really pleased about that and there's this CD coming out. It's going to be an interesting Christmas.

Point of View: 'I try to make the animal catch life and have breath'

CM: In your stories, nature, the environment, animals play such an important part and often you'll take the point of view of the animal, like Joey, like Toto, How do you approach that?
MM: With a bit of a joy in my heart really. I've done it with all these poems for 'Carnival of the Animals'. Quite a lot of people just write poems about animals out there. Most of these poems, in fact all of them, I've written from the inside of the animal, looking outwards.
CM: So how do you achieve that?
MM: Well, I suppose the truth of the matter is that these poems are really about us, they're not really about the animals at all, but don't tell anyone else that. Each one is a take on how it is we treat and use and love and abuse and exploit animals. They're not just sweet little poems, they've all got a bit of an edge to them. In the Saint-Saëns poems there are two about a donkey. One of them is a wild donkey, very proud of his freedom, and the other is a working donkey, who does not like to be despised because he's working. He gets whipped, he gets beaten and there are flies to deal with but he's up. And at the end of the day, he says, 'When you next see a donkey, you're looking at a diva. No one else sings like a donkey.' I try to make the animal catch life and have breath but through a conversation with us.

Ted Hughes: 'he brought not just expertise but prestige to children's writing'

CM: I like that. Thinking about poetry, I was going to ask about your friendship with Ted Hughes and Seán Rafferty. How important were those friendships to you as a writer?
MM: Huge, they were huge. It was a tiny little village and there were three of us that were writers. Hughes was a great, great writer. Rafferty was a great writer but comparatively unknown and I was writing children's books. We were having dinner once a week and we'd meet at the pub and the number of dinners we had was no one's business. We really got to know each other well. Seán and Ted would give us poems and I'd give them stories. They were both mentors for me, there's no doubt about that and a source of encouragement when you get down. Finally, we were

encouraging each other. They talked, the two of them, in depth about Yeats and people that they'd known and read and loved. They talked a kind of a conversation which was highly literary. We had one evening at our cottage, it was just extraordinary, where there was Stephen Spender, Basil Bunting, Seamus Heaney, Ted Hughes, all round the table. You just sat there listening.

But then, in times of difficulty, when I was stuck at one particular point, I got a lot of advice from Ted. When 'War Horse' didn't win the Whitbread Prize, he took me out. We had a lovely trip out to see bookshops in Bideford and he sat me down for tea. He didn't say a word about it all day until teatime and then he sat me down and said, 'Oh yeah, about last night, the Whitbread stuff, don't pay any attention. Prizes are nothing. They're not good for you if you win them. They're not good for you if you lose them. Just write the next book at forget it.' He said, ''War Horse' is a great story. You'll write a greater one.' So he did that kind of double-edged thing of encouraging you when you needed it most. He was a very genuinely kind man and he really cared about young writers – and that's what I was; I was in my thirties. He was very involved in the Arvon Foundation, getting young people to write. He was passionate about it. He judged the Daily Mirror Children's Writing Competition for years and years and got colleagues like Seamus Heaney particularly to come in. He brought not just expertise but prestige to children's writing. Of course, he and I between us started the Children's Laureate thing and that was after a dinner at his house. We'd probably drunk too much and I said, 'Well, you're a flamin' Poet Laureate, why can't we have a Children's Laureate too? That'll lift the spirits of everyone in children's literature.' He stopped and said, 'Yes, that's a good idea. Who will we go to?' and he made a list of all the people to go to: Waterstone, someone royal who could launch it. By the time the first Children's Laureate was appointed, which was Quentin Blake, Ted Hughes had died, which was sad, so he never saw it come to fruition. He'd be thrilled to bits now because we've had ten.

CM: You were the third.

Children's Literature: 'they're actually cracking good stories and we love them'

MM: I was the third. It was a flippant remark to start with but it is what children's books always needed. It's been provided by many, many terrific writers and also the times, I think. People have understood that we enrich children's lives, give them life chances which they wouldn't have otherwise and that books bring you knowledge and understanding. That's *spoken* now. There are certain people like Philip Pullman and J K Rowling, whose names are part of the adult world as well and that's really important because some adults tend to patronise children and children's writers. 'Oh, it's just for children.' Well, if you think now about the writers out there; when the theatres were working, you could walk around the West End and a good third to a half of all the productions were from children's books. People have finally realised that they're actually cracking good stories and we love them. That was

never the case before. The Children's Laureate has helped that because for two years of an illustrator's life or a writer's life or a poet's life, they give themselves to this idea that it's important so that parents and teachers and education ministers and politicians have realised that literature is not for the few.
CM: So that kind of title then is important and useful, important because it's useful?
MM: Yes. It's very important if you use it right.
CM: How do you use it right?

Stories: 'Story-making, storytelling should be a part of every day of a child's life'

MM: Well, everyone uses it differently, Quentin Blake, when he was Children's Laureate, very deliberately set it up to show illustration as one form of art which is usually hidden round a corner somewhere, but he went to the National Gallery and you had his pictures interspersed with great art and it *is* great art. There's that awful thing, that it can't be because it's only for children - but it *is* actually. Time after time now, that's what people have done. They've taken their own fix, I suppose, on what was needed. The ownership of books was very important to Anne Fine. She decided that it was very important that kids owned books because it's something you can take home and it becomes *you*. I did the making of stories and the enjoyment of stories, the listening to stories. So, I travelled the world, literally the world, Russia to South Africa, reading stories to people and to children and to students and to teachers, trying to inculcate in people a huge enthusiasm for telling stories to children. I'm still on my mission. My mission is that every child should have half an hour at school at the end of the day. From 3 – 3.30pm in every Primary School, they should be reading a story or being read a story or writing a story. Story-making, storytelling should be a part of every day of a child's life. Only in that way do you inculcate in them a love of books and of course it's got to be inculcated into the teachers as well. They do that at college, so we're working on it. It's work in progress.
CM: So you would say that's your principal responsibility?

Libraries: 'they are as important…as hospitals'

MM: Oh completely. I think for all children's writers, that's what we do. We're doing all we possibly can to spread the word. When you close a library, you shut off a child's mind. That's effectively what you do. They are as important, and I sense this is a big statement, as hospitals. Hospitals are dealing with the body, libraries are dealing with the mind. If you shut off a library, you are shutting off, for those who need it most, their source of stories, It is through stories that you find out about yourself, it improves your mental health, your self-esteem. It helps you climb out of loneliness. All these things can happen in a library. That is just as important as getting yourself checked out at a hospital. Just at the moment, I know we're absolutely focused on getting ourselves healthy but we are going to learn, if we haven't learned already, that the health of the mind is not just about taking a pill or going to tell everyone your troubles. It is about understanding yourself through stories, through poetry and the life of others and the world around you. All this helps you look beyond yourself. That's the richness of it.

2021 Publication: 'Over The Fields And Far Away' (HarperCollins)

CM: In your email you said you were mid-novel.
MM: That was just to put you off. I say that to everyone and then I heard that you lived locally and so that was alright. I was trying to avoid another Zoom or something.
No, I've finished a series of short stories, the working title of which is 'Over The Fields And Far Away' and it's a story of kids who come to the farm but in nine stories. They're all set on the farms where the children come to from the cities. It's the story of their lives and what the farm means to them and each one is different – different animal, different child, different place. I'm very passionate about it because our project is closed down at the moment. Because of the pandemic, we can't have children. So the charity is looking into a big black hole, like all charities and businesses are. It's going to be some while before the children can come down again so we're raising funds like crazy. That's what my wife has been doing because we just need to keep going until the children come back. We had the same with the Foot and Mouth disease, we were shut down for nine months. The children come, they pay something; it's not much but it keeps us going. We're a charity anyway, so we've got to go out there and raise funds which is what we've been doing. Part of the reason I've done these stories is to raise funds for 'Farms for City Children'.
CM: Who is the publisher?
MM: HarperCollins
CM: So that's 'Over the Fields and Far Away' published by HarperCollins, thank you.
MM: That'll be next year.
CM: So, what's next for you then?
MM: You sound just like my publisher!
CM: Oh, do I really? Oh sorry.

What's Next: 'I'm heading for a pause now'

MM: What's next? I think the truth is I'm going to write a novella of some sort, I'm not quite sure what it'll be. I'm thinking about 3 or 4 different subjects but at the present moment, well, I've been writing all these retellings of Shakespeare, which was wonderful – I mean just to live with the stories of Shakespeare for three months is just terrific, very good therapy. With that done and with my stories done, I'm looking to write a novella but I'm heading for a pause now. I've got another book coming out. I've got so much coming out but I've got a book coming out next year which is the last novel I wrote and is set in Greece. I'm not sure what it's going to be called yet but it's all written and done. It's about Ithaca and what I'm quite pleased about is that it's the story of the life of one girl, Elena. She grows up in Australia, knowing she's Greek, which a lot of people do in Melbourne, and she comes back and finds her home and also someone who visits her from time to time in Australia but lives on Ithaca. She finds out through this woman really the whole story not just of her life, this aunty of hers, but also about the history of that whole island, through the eyes and the life of this woman. Anyway, it's all done but they keep wanting to change the title. Well, that's grand. I hope that's what you needed.

CM: Oh, it is. Thank you so much, this has been wonderful, absolutely wonderful. Thank you. Thank you from all of us.

The Write Life with Clare Morris

A Writerly Alchemy

When Robert of Chester completed his translation of 'The Book of the Composition of Alchemy' in 1144, he introduced alchemy to 12th century Europe and with it such words as alcohol, carboy, elixir and athanor for which there were no Latin equivalents. In his act of translation, he gave us something new. In my previous editorial, I used the phrase 'a writerly alchemy' to describe how we spark off each other's ideas as we write and create. In attempting to transmute base metal into gold, alchemists refine and purify again and again, hoping to produce the quintessence, that mysterious fifth entity thought to be latent in all things. As writers, we draft and redraft, endeavouring to convey the pure essence of the experience. I have returned to the same phrase in this editorial in the hope that we will be able to delve deeper into our own 'Write Life' – and in doing so capture the essence of our craft.

When, as a young girl, I discovered the word quintessence, I thought it the most remarkable word I had ever read or heard. For me, bizarrely, it conjured up an image of an enormous Bakewell tart, its quintessence being the cherry on the top. This could well have stemmed from the advertising slogan that Mr Kipling makes 'exceedingly good cakes'. I reasoned that he obviously had the quintessence in his sights when he created his Cherry Bakewells.

Fast forward to 2020 and the joy of discovery has been swamped by the daily task of getting by and staying safe in the 'new normal '. So, where is the magic now? Well, the truth is that it is where it has always been: hiding in plain sight, in the words we use, recall and create to reveal the world. If somewhere along the way, we have momentarily lost the connection, the four pieces I have selected for this issue will help us to re-establish that link. They each respond to the wonder of words in different ways and remind us about the charm of it all.

Sophia Kouidou-Giles is a regular contributor to The Write Life, offering powerful insights into the task of translating. She often discusses the processes we use in order to make each translation ring as truly as it did in the original version. In 'The Alchemy of Words' she explores the way we hope to transform base ideas into gold when we write. In citing the Muses, she transports us to Greece, the land of her birth, reflecting on the endless permutations that '[transform] our ordinary souls into the magic world of books.' She reminds us of Homer's gift for words. Whether the Iliad and the Odyssey are the works of one writer or several, the wonder still remains.

I have been delighted to welcome Michael Paul Hogan to The Write Life pages. His work always sparkles with energy, reflecting the sheer breadth of his experience as a poet, journalist, fiction writer and literary essayist. In 'Tsundoku and the Art of Infinite Reading' he deftly summarises both the joy and the torment in our love of books. His subtle focus on the undervalued art of listening is a telling point and one to be explored further. He observes, 'We are a strange people, a noisy people. We praise a man for being a great orator; we rarely bestow equal stature on a great listener.' How true! His story within a story, with the lightest of post-modernist touches, reflects the infinity of reading.

Dominic Fisher is another regular contributor to The Write Life, whose series 'Notes From The Allotment' offers readers a delightful mix of wry humour, perceptive poetry criticism and pertinent gardening tips as he engages in conversation with visiting poets. That they are all dead reflects his constant concern to keep The Write Life on the legal side of copyright laws more than anything else. Knowing we were about to visit his allotment shed, he has generously whipped up a tempting alchemical salad, remembering some of the visitors he had welcomed previously and revealing those still to knock on his shed door. 'And rising up out of the clay and humus in the long evenings are other fragments, invented poets, inventions of poets by the same poet, and poets who never existed.' Just breathe in the smell of that damp earth and believe!

Kevin Kling's first contribution to The Write Life, 'Staying Up All Night' gave words to our grief at George Floyd's murder. With over 2,500 likes on Facebook, it clearly spoke to us all. His piece 'Questions and Answers' neatly brings us back to Greek Literature once more with its discussion of the weaving of metaphor and sequence to create cloaks of immortality. Among the cacophony of bird calls, car horns and laundromats, we are offered the silent gift of a blind goatherd's smile.

The blind goatherd in Kevin's story resonates throughout literature. Homer and Tiresias are perhaps the more obvious connections, both blessed with an insight that saw beyond their blindness. Tiresias' prophetic gifts must have been intensified too by the knowledge gained from the seven years he lived as a woman. But then the goatherd surely has subtle echoes of Caedmon, the earliest named English poet. An illiterate herdsman who lived in 7th century Northumbria, he feared singing and speaking in front of others until he had a dream that encouraged him to find his voice.

The first word he uttered when relating his poem to the monks was 'Nú' – Now. Now he could put his former shyness behind him. Now he had a poem. Now he could sing. Now he was free. Now. What a wonderful starting point. All he needed was someone to listen to him and write it down.

On Cape Clear island, Kevin tells us, birds find refuge and we find answers to questions we have not even asked. Everything has some sort of connection if you listen hard enough.

And perhaps that is ultimately what is at the heart of our writerly alchemy – to write and to read well we must learn to listen too.

Nú. Now.

Clare Morris.
Write Life Editor

The Alchemy of Words by Sophia Kouidou-Giles

At the end of the day, here is what we writers do: we make magic when we delve into plots, set the stage, draw scenes, choose words, linger in the past or visualize the future. We levitate, turning into alchemists of the soul. We take ink and draft words. We take clay and give it shape. We take lead and turn it into gold.

Although we are common, everyday folk, our quest leads us to the temple to sacrifice at the altar of time and we pray for gifts and inspiration. Born observers, we set the camera lens wide to begin the story and settle into a draft, selecting a setting, be it the sea, the desert or the moon, as we breathe life into our characters. Starting from ground zero, we weigh each word and engage in creating order. True citizens of this world, we serve. We sing for the deaf, paint for the blind, soften the pain of the wounded, speak our truth and fashion visions for tomorrow.

The storyteller's universe is huge, so we have to chunk it down to manageable pieces and when the ground underneath our feet feels firm and confidence builds, we mold drafts, observe, review, taste and finally settle on a composition that borrows from the four elements of nature: earth, air, fire and water. In the confines of our cauldron, we brew our story.

I would be a fool to try to list all the ingredients, modest, rich or exquisite involved in this enterprise. Devoted students and readers, we make sense out of chaos, standing on the shoulders of those who have gone before us. Our ultimate teacher is reading, writing, and writing some more. Each time, the practice itself reveals to us another aspect to store in the depot of our craft.

Driven and inspired by disparate elements, we weave together fiction, non-fiction, poetry, and drama as we invoke the Muses, who reign over literature, science and art and channel their words onto the page. There are nine and they are daughters of Zeus and Mnemosyne; we commune with them, sacrificing hours and days, dedicating ourselves to the cult of writing. They stand tall over us, taking turns, whispering, and we rush to record each word.

This ancient line up suggests mirrors, the distinct forms of art that are present and reflect creativity in each other. Euterpe, the Muse of music, swings along a tune as Terpsichore choreographs the seduction of the reader and we record. Bodies swirl to the rhythms of the melody, but hold still, because dance is sculpture that stands still for a moment when we stop action to capture the intensity of the scene. Erato fashions poetic lyrics and Calliope moves the plot into epic dimensions in gifted hands, like Homer's. And the parade continues to unfold as endless permutations of words achieve the alchemy transforming our ordinary souls into the magic world of books.

Tsundoku and the Art of Infinite Reading by Michael Paul Hogan

Tsundoku: The compulsion to buy more books than one can ever possibly hope to have a sufficient lifetime to read.

'Even when reading is impossible, the presence of books acquired produces such an ecstasy that the buying of more books than one can read is nothing less than the soul reaching towards infinity'

Edward Newton,
Collector of English & American Literature (1864 – 1940).

It is typical of the Japanese to create a noun to name that which no-one previously knew existed, and equally typical that such a noun should combine metaphysics and fine art, but in respect of the Newton quote, I know just what he means, and if I did not share his almost mystical belief that the buying of more and more books is like adding bricks to a tower in which one can hide from Death, I would think it a wildly romantic hyperbole – and one extremely difficult for a non-bibliophile to understand. But, in accordance with Scott Fitzgerald's definition of a well-balanced mind, I am able to hold two completely contradictory ideas at the same time and, despite a perfectly sound and scientifically-based respect for the limits of human mortality, remain peculiarly convinced that my time on earth will magically expand to accommodate each new (albeit usually second-hand) book I all too frequently buy. In short, like Zeno's arrow, I am destined to be aimed correctly but never to arrive…

Newton wasn't just a famous book-collector, he actually wrote a book, and the wonderful irony is that this book, **The Amenities of Book-Collecting and Kindred Affections** by A. Edward Newton, The Atlantic Monthly Press, Boston, 1918, is, despite its rather ponderous title, as worthy of being collected as many of the books people do actually collect. The chapter on Oscar Wilde alone is worth the admission price, and is as well-balanced and critically sound as the work of any contemporary scholar. It is one of those warm, wise, witty volumes that makes you think the author would've been a pleasure to know – and he also possesses an extraordinary, and quite unexpected, gift for deadpan humour. Almost every page has a quotable passage, and there are 355 pp to choose from, but here are a few, taken more or less at random (and they're often at their best when they have only a tangential relationship to books). –

'First editions are scarce; tenth editions are scarcer.'

'Pets die too, in spite of constant care – perhaps by reason of it. To quiet a teething dog I once took him, her, it, to my room for the night and slept soundly. Next morning, I found that the dog had committed suicide by jumping out of the window.'

'We should buy our books as we buy our clothes, not only to cover our nakedness but to embellish us; and we should buy more books and fewer clothes.'

'The fog and soot of London soon give the newest building an appearance of age, and mercifully bring it into harmony with its surroundings.'

'Golf has taken the place of books. I know that it takes time and lots of money. I do not play the game myself, but I have a son who does. Perhaps when I am his age, I will feel that I can afford it.'

'The two great events of Nelson's life were his meeting with Lady Emma Hamilton and his meeting with the French.'

'The Brontës were geniuses undoubtably, especially Emily, but one would hardly select the author of 'Wuthering Heights' as a companion for a social evening.'

As is evident, I like Newton enormously, but he also somehow manages to bring into focus the relationship between reader and writer; or better still, between reading and writing. I was once in conversation with a poet and editor who said, 'I want to live in a world where people write.' My knee-jerk response was, 'There's books enough already to fill a thousand libraries. I want to live in a world where people *read*.'

I might well have gone on to say that for me the burning of the Great Library at Alexandria in 48 BC was the greatest tragedy in antiquity, far worse than the combined destructions of Carthage and Troy.

We are a strange people, a noisy people. We praise a man for being a great orator; we rarely bestow equal stature on a great listener. Likewise, with the printed word: If I ask you who are the world's ten greatest contemporary writers, you will swiftly bend yourself to the task, arguing with your friends and colleagues about who should be included, who not. But if I were to ask you who were the world's ten greatest readers, you would be confused and disappointed by the very nature of the question – and I would certainly not anticipate much in the way of an answer. You would eventually counter that reading is a silent, solitary pursuit, it does not lend itself to be appreciated by others; cannot be qualified or quantified. I quite agree. I would then admit that my question was ironic and intended to make you think about the nature of the question itself rather than any possible (or, indeed, impossible) answer. And after a certain amount of Socratic dialectic we would reach the point I always intended we should reach: the civilised world can live without writers, but it cannot live without readers. If already so many books exist that the word tsundoku can be coined, then the world has no need of any more. It has instead great need of intelligent thoughtful people to read and appreciate the many wonderful books we already have – and equally intelligent and committed people to build and maintain the libraries and collections that will ensure those books are preserved and made available for generations to come.

I once heard a story that may not be entirely irrelevant. It is in fact a story within a story, and it was told to me by a wise old man in a land very far away –

We are a strange people, a remote and distant people, who believe that reading is the highest form of literary endeavour, whose home lies beyond Mount Fuji and beyond the Sea of Endless Ice. A man or a woman who has read a thousand poems is allowed a sheet of parchment upon which to write a single haiku, thus maintaining the balance and harmony between that which has been written and that which can be read. A man or a woman who has read a thousand stories is entitled to transcribe the events of a (fictional) day. Thus we aim, within a further nine generations, to bestow upon our elders the ultimate gift of Eternal Sleep in The Land Where All Books Have Been Read. However, even in our well-ordered land a dissident voice is not always unheard and one night, not so long ago, an unauthorised story appeared, nailed to the Shrine of the Silent Reader. It was brief (do we not value brevity?) and went something like this –

As the first old man to have bought and read every book ever written or printed, the first man to be released from the curse of Infinite Reading, turned his back on his home and his family and set one foot on the bridge that separated our village from the City of Eternal Sleep, a girl, his grand-daughter, broke free from her mother and ran towards him with a sheet of paper in her hand, shouting, "So-Fu! So-Fu! I have written a story for you. Please come back and read it!"

It was signed **TSUNDOKU**. May his name burn in the lava of a thousand volcanoes and never know a day of peace!

Alchemical Salad by Dominic Fisher

Allotments are magical places. You put shiny piebald beans in the ground and then up come more in fat green purses. Then you put some black dots into the darkness and lettuces emerge. Then there's rhubarb – dump a ton of manure on it in the autumn and green fig-leaf shapes as big as aprons rise on rude pink stalks as early as January.

And if it's not over-extending the metaphor that's sneaking up on us from behind the sweetcorn, poems are like that too in many ways. Actually, I'm not sure how garlic fits into this as it doesn't grow from seed, but still, you put a clove into soil and it turns into a head there. Also the beds are like verses, carefully dug line by line. Heavy feeders such as cabbages or potatoes go in one bed, medium feeders such as carrots go in the next, and light feeders such as peas and beans go in the third. Each year they move up one bed. This rotation makes the whole plot practically a villanelle.

Maybe that's why, on this particular plot, it's not just veg that comes up out of the ground. As you may know, we've had all sorts of dead poets visiting, mostly not suitably dressed or very well versed in horticultural practice.

Some have been, though. Emily Dickinson certainly knew her onions. She had a lovely voice, and it was quite soothing going round with her comparing British and American varieties. She asked some very perceptive questions about potatoes and was especially interested in the Pink Fir Apples. To call her 'down to earth' is a bit obvious, but she really was. She was well aware, for example, of the propensity of rats to get in the compost bins. Or as she put it:

> The Rat is the concisest Tenant.
> He pays no Rent.
> Repudiates the Obligation –
> On Schemes intent

and, I would add, scrabbles about under the shed.

William Wordsworth was hopeless. He didn't know one end of a spade from the other, and his shoes weren't up to the job in any case. To be fair, he was as responsible for the centrality of nature in English language poetry as anyone. The following are the opening lines to the *Childhood and School-time* section of *The Prelude*.

> Fair seed-time had my soul, and I grew up
> Foster'd alike by beauty and by fear:
> Much favour'd in my birthplace, and no less
> In that beloved Vale to which, erelong
> I was transplanted.

It's difficult now not to see such language as archaic and the imagery as very familiar, but well over two hundred years ago his use of what was in many ways plain everyday language was revolutionary, and the idea of the soul or person as a plant would have been shocking to many. But then it was his sister Dorothy who was the actual gardener. When they were in the Quantocks with the Coleridges it was she who grew any food. When they went on their long walks it was she who took notes. And when she visited our plot she was full of very sound advice. She seems to have been content to walk in her brother's shadow, but she was the observer and it was she whose hands were in the soil.

Allen Ginsberg and Dylan Thomas were both more fun than the Wordsworths, but they weren't great gardeners. It was baking hot when Ginsberg showed up, but he took an interest, particularly in the poppies (which incidentally seed themselves, and in our climate are only psychotropic if you are dead). It was dripping wet when Thomas came and he showed little interest at all and was somewhat disparaging about the shed (which admittedly *is* a bit untidy and creaky). William Carlos Williams did help plant the potatoes, although he kept wanting to eulogise the wheelbarrow.

I think Sappho turned up once. It was hard to know, I can't remember how long ago it was, and listening to her was a bit like trying to reassemble the bits of pottery you dig up from time to time. It was disturbingly catching.

DF: How far have you –
S : Leave Crete and come to us
DF: I'm sorry, did you –
S : I hear that Andromeda – has put a torch to your heart

(translations Mary Barnard)

Perhaps the strangest so far to come up out of the ground in the middle of the raspberries was Fernando Pessoa. He was an early twentieth century Portugese poet whose surname translates as 'person,' or into French possibly as 'no one,' who split himself into several poets. These alter egos of his he called 'heteronyms,' one of these being himself. One of his heteronyms was a Frenchman Jean Seul, and another an English poet he called Richard Search. Fortunately, Pessoa arrived in person rather than as Search. Search's work is not, I think, as good as that of the others, being written in a mannered and antiquated English. All the same, and luckily for me, Pessoa's English was excellent. My favourite persona of his is Alberto Caeiro, who for someone who arguably never existed is very interesting on nature.

> Salad*
>
> What a medley of Nature fills my plate!
> My sisters the plants,
> The companions of springs, the saints
> No one prays to ...
>
> And they're cut and brought to our table,
> And in the hotels the noisy guests
> Arrive with their strapped-up blankets
> And casually order "Salad,"

Without thinking that they're requiring Mother Earth
To give her freshness and her first-born children,
Her very first green words,
The first living and gleaming things
That Noah saw
When the waters subsided and the hilltops emerged
All drenched and green,
And in the sky where the dove appeared
The rainbow started to fade ...

(translation Richard Zenith, 2006)

[*confusingly 'Salad' seems to be the first verse and not the title. Caeiro's work didn't have titles]

And rising up out of the clay and humus in the long evenings are other fragments, invented poets, inventions of poets by the same poet, and poets who never existed. There are pieces of the ghosts of poets, vapours and misquotations of them, and poets no one has heard of – some who have stars singing in their bloodstreams, others simply printer ink. Neighbouring plot-holders think it's my compost bins, and that I talk to myself, but then so do they.

It's a wonder any work gets done. But the alchemy of sunlight and compost brings salad out of the dark nonetheless, carrots, parsnips, and pumpkins.

NB

Sappho translations by Mary Barnard from *The Penguin Book of Women Poets*, 1980

Pessoa translation by Richard Zenith from *Fernando Pessoa: A little Larger Than the Entire Universe*, Penguin Classics, 2006, © the translator

Questions and Answers by Kevin Kling

I feel stories are about questions more than answers. We tell the same stories as our ancestors because we have the same questions. Where do we come from before life, where do we go after death, what is funny, edible, sacred?

Often times more important than an answer is to know that we aren't alone.

We give our lives value through our struggles and our struggles voice through our stories.

John Berger said 'Stories bring meaning to experience.'

The Ancient Greeks believed that a story worked like a loom in that vertically ran the metaphor, horizontally ran the sequence, and where they came together they wove invisible yarns for their cloaks of immortality.

On the island of Cape Clear, in the south of Ireland, a festival happens that is regarded as one of the best in the world by audiences and storytellers alike. The festival is online this year and again features some of the best storytellers the world has to offer. I travelled there in 2000 and wrote this story.

Cape Clear island lies off of the southern-most tip of Ireland. In many ways it has the feel of a typical Irish countryside, whitewashed cottages with thatched roofs, the roads not wide enough for two cars to pass, thick hedgerows and rock walls dating back hundreds of years. On the highest point of this tiny island there are ancient ruins, rock formations, spires and sanctuaries that align the landscape with the stars. These spires point to similar structures in South America and Mongolia. At night the Cape Clear sky unleashes a view of the heavens unlike any other. In a Cape Clear pub Jerry, a bright-eyed man from Limerick, decides we should be friends.

The next day Jerry is walking with me to have ice cream.

As we make our way we are surrounded by a most disturbing sound. It's the birds. A cacophony of calls, whistles, chirps, cackles.

Jerry explains that, because of Cape Clear's location, birds from all of the major flyways come here. Africa, Europe, North and South America even Asia. Blown off course, this is the first land they see. These birds have decided that after being blown across the ocean, 'that's it, I'm not going back out there', and have made it home. Cape Clear is an ornithologist's paradise. I see parrots, sparrows, crows, hawks, robins, finches.

The ice cream is made by a local man who is blind and a goatherder. Incredible ice cream, Chocolate or vanilla, that's all he makes. "And be careful," says Jerry, "every once in a while, a small stone."

The birds outside are particularly active. We have to shout to be heard. The goatherder smiles and I'm reminded of my friend John, from back in the States.

John has perfect pitch, if you hear a car horn honk he can tell you what key it's in. John is also blind, a Christian, schizophrenic and gay. He said years ago his head was so full of conflicted voices, he thought several times of suicide. Then one day he was in a laundromat. All the machines were going, washers and driers. Inside that chaotic laundromat John said he could hear patterns. He figured that if there were patterns, connections, in that place, then there must be in his conflicted life as well. He hasn't thought of suicide since.

I sit in the goatherder's shack.

He smiles and Jerry looks at me with those intense eyes of his. I'm being given a gift. I don't understand it yet but I do know that sometimes life gives you answers before the questions.

International Poets & Poetry in Translation with Clara Burghelea

Editorial

Reading as an activity is private, though can take place almost anywhere: in an inviting library, in one's cozy nook or outdoors. Reading for Issue 43 began and ended in a changed world where socializing has been reinvented and spending time outside our homes has to unfold under certain circumstances. The summer of 2020 will remain in our collective memory as that of no hugs, no shows, no visits, no reading performances, no travelling. How does poetry reading fit this unexpected, heart-breaking global picture?

The answer lies within the large number of submissions we received and what an incredible opportunity again to learn about the joys and parameters of putting together yet another exquisite issue. This Issue 43 in particular has meant a strong collaboration with the other editors and such exchange of opinions and love has found its place in the quality of the included work.

So, kind reader, ready yourself for excursions in various forms – prose poem, haiku, free verse, historical poetry – and visceral content, mood and mode and playful voice. Discover our featured poet, Cătălina Florina Florescu, who praises the mother figure in her poem "Hatching the Death Egg" where birth is portrayed in reverse, from dying bed to ovum: "The woman is hatching/ a hallow egg:/barely moving/she looks for/a bed/to die". Her poems on motherhood and the dynamics of married life are echoed in the poetry of Viviana Fiorentino.

In her poem, "Road lines", the relationship between mother and daughter is compared to a road trip that both gives space for careless window gazing and hurtful conversation: "And while you point/where air scatters /more light, for the sky kindness or the sun obstinacy,/edges/ align between us. Love for you. The weight of your/ heart /before I feel it. /Impossible crossroads where you and I are mother."

Viviana Fiorentino's poem "Belonging" beautifully resonates with Josie Di Sciascio-Andrews's prose poem "City of Dreams" where a city seduces its newly-arrived individuals with its glowing light and the promise of "wading into the greater sea of the collective, claiming us citizen unto itself." In this sea of bodies, the body is equally visible and invisible. In her other poem, "La Chasse Galerie", inspired by the legend of Flying Canoe from Québec, Canada, the suffering body is healed for "nature sanctifies me, / Even as the icy scissor of winter/Cuts at my face, my toes, my bones. / Pain numbs. In the velour darkness /Of its' gnathic clench, I yield to the holy."

Moreover, the (image of the body under siege finds its way in Margot Saffer's poem "Prayer for the Fallen (of Marikana)" written back in 2012 in honor of the miners killed during a strike at a mine in the Marikana region of South Africa. In the poet's words "this is still an unresolved, painful issue for those who lost loved ones, as well as for the entire mining industry and its current and historical state ties.16 August will be the anniversary."

Reading and poetry continue to be an important part of our lives, those of us who believe words can unshackle, purge, sing, connect, remain the ink blood of our daily interactions, and a measure of our humane ability for endless hope.

Thank you for taking time to enjoy the words of these fearless, well-established and emerging female poets alike.

Clara Burghelea
International/ Poetry in Translation Editor

Poetry by Cătălina Florina Florescu

Hatching the Death Egg
In memoriam, to mother

The woman is hatching
a hallow egg:
barely moving
she looks for
a bed
to die.

It's not the one where she made love.
It's not her mother's either.
It's her daughters'.

She stays there awhile --
hatching is
almost over.

The woman is
a child
playing
again
until the end.

Portrait in Syllables & Mixed Languages

> *"i found god in myself & i loved her*
>   *I loved her fiercely –"*
>   Ntozake Shange

Ive never been good at cooking,
& here i am: mixin' ancestries and languages—
Romanian in itself is an adulterous Romance language
full with words from others
bc they have overstayed their welcome: Romans, Turks, Russians
they came there like a river carries its mud and sorrows
or maybe

I dunno, maybe, bc the country's compass doesnt turn Romance
left and right
and up and down.
We let travelers, *străini*, flâneurs

be with us & offered them our proverbial
pâine cu sare.

Which reminds me that I've started cookin' smth,
no idea what!
I move backwards as foolproof mnemonic device:
and I remember that i was cooking

myself, reinventing,
the body does that – the last, desperate shot at fame,

only IDC,
fame is no biggie for me.
I need to make sure that what I do does not ever
erase my birthmark:
it's not a burden of being white but of being (a) woman
who fights with God and his alleged apple.

But maybe God is a woman who wanted to cook a pie
turned her head for a split second and saw a bite into
a fallen apple.

If woman is a fugitive that's
bc, like language, she's never
fully done --
necoaptă.

Raw, in Reverse

Playing with a fork on
a barely touched meal
he sighed.

She didn't say a word--
Took a sip of water.

He tried again
to eat.
"This tastes like shrapnel."

A war lasts longer after it's declared
over. She looked for something

underneath the table.
"I need air."

She put on a diver's mask.

By the time she was at the door
the whole place disintegrated under water. On second thought,
A postcard from a distant galaxy.

Poetry by Josie Di Sciascio-Andrews

La Chasse Galerie

Black night. The lake is a mirror
Of stars ensorcelled in glass.

Swaying on the bruised rim,
The moon is a lit lantern,

And the water, a quick-leap weave
Of brindled pickerel slipping away.

Long ago, the legend says,
Men in a canoe drowned here.

Sold their souls to the devil himself,
To see their families one more time.

What I wouldn't give to do the same!
But though I wish and beg, no ghosts appear.

Only the salt-like patterns of fixed
Luminous points cluster my gaze,

As big dipper spills a toboggan of advice
On the serpentine wing of the cosmos.

Although I stand in a gorge of doubts
And griefs, nature sanctifies me,

Even as the icy scissor of winter
Cuts at my face, my toes, my bones.

Pain numbs. In the velour darkness
Of its' gnathic clench, I yield to the holy.

City of Dreams

We skimmed the center of the city from a circular railway. On its golden radius, a dazzle of white light breathed from the pale-hued dwellings, mesmerizing our gaze. From liminal perimeters, the city glowed, a chandelier of candles on a pristine altar. Our locomotive rimmed the station's threshold, braking slowly into alabaster, low-hanging clouds. Suitcase in hand, we stepped out of the train's vapors into the milling crowd. Drawn by the city's magic, we merged into its essence, each segment of our individual selves wading into the greater sea of the collective, claiming us citizen unto itself.

*(La Chasse Galerie is a legend from Québec, Canada.)

Poetry by Margot Saffer

Prayer for the Fallen (of Marikana)
                         with acknowledgements to Louis MacNeice

You are already dead, why hear you?
Come with your *pangas* and your *sjamboks*, machetes and
    your blame.

You are already dead, congratulate you.
You paid for bread with blood, beer with bones,
    lungs last coughed, coal cut and gold grated, daily-indexed and platinum-fated,
        paid for your livelihood with your life.

You are already dead, respect you
With prayers to con-soul you, monuments to visit you, photographs
    to know you, politicians to claim you, memorials and a national holiday
        in wintertime to live you.

You are already dead, exploit you
For the fuels that flow at your flint, your yeses
    when they agree you, your actions when they define you,
        your time when they mine you,
            your life when they murder by means of your
        hands, your orders when they obey you.

You are already dead, why hear you?
Come meet the men with guns who think they are different from you,
    the men who will kill you.

You are already dead, remind you
What you died fighting for, what they protected when
    their fear shot at your numbers,
        a week after Women's Day, two months and thirty-six years
          after Soweto,
    those who have made you a cog in a machine, pickaxes and guns, a thing with
        one face, a thing, the cops and the miners, the unions, and
    Commissions, paid in platinum.

You are already dead, who were you?
Cover your bodies from the shots and the flashes,
    dead
        you become no longer things, people
            with names and faces, lovers and children, dreams
      for one day, if first
  you did not die.

You were men who were killed by men.
You did your job and they did theirs.

[The cheque is in the mail, gold-plated, platinum-fated.]

17 August, 2012

Waking News
(for Liviu Sigler)
I stir and I stir
insoluble irony
into my coffee

Poetry by Viviana Fiorentino

Road lines

You, mother, driving, me at your side -, we talk as I watch
edges

aligning with the road. Fragments of landscape in dots of trees and shrubs. You speak
softly

of ending and loss. I turn to the other window, rain falling in the other direction,
out

where the wind tilts things with no attention. To you mother, who
I love,

I talk of bags I forgot, and the books I haven't read. Yet rain falls
faster

in lines slanting the world underneath. Coincidences have weight. I wanted to tell you

– while you talk of deities' pity for us, your fate, my chance, our possibilities -

but you want to pay for those parcels I forgot. You won't turn into
slip roads

we could take. And while you point
where air scatters

more light, for the sky kindness or the sun obstinacy,
edges

align between us. Love for you. The weight of your

heart
before I feel it.

Impossible crossroads where you and I are mother.

Belonging

I – BETWEEN

Lines of smoking chimneys, distances go silent.

An empty sky doesn't move, it crushes the movements below.
Thinking of us, walking side by side
on the main avenue, in the city where I was born.
A spring of years ago, under tall sycamores.
My shoulder close to your shoulder, our feet on different countries
as it is also for our memories.

You emerged at night, from centuries of difficult sleep.
I came to the edge of your bed, the pillow forming a frame around your head,
the uncombed hair impressed on the linen like an ink sketch
both knees on the ground, I begged you.
Denying a story is like a light going off.

A door opened on our dark house, the old house with no smell of coffee.
The dining room still, dissolving every street outside.
You left with a grief, I know, hating me caring for you.
You told me, you stood by the door
listening to the silence, growing backwards
staring at the place where we left unused objects down at the tidal time,
recovered, tainted, dusty.

You stepped back, moonlight drawing you from darkness.

I don't know, what is not and what has been
where I come from, edges by edges
when I arrive at the borders between me and you.

What's the name of this bizarre country
the strange avenue of belonging?

II – A PHOTO

An old picture
with you mother
and a red bicycle

You bent towards me
whispering in my ear

I didn't like smiling in photos,
yet I was smiling to you.

My chin in your palm
holding delicate the weight of bodies.

My straw hat
tall trees and anemones
our old garden.

Words I don't know anymore.

Love bent you
it folded even time
into an origami flower.

Collapsed in a blind corner of the photo
words lay preserved
whispered
scrumped
from the ruins of time.

We smiled most mornings.

The camera didn't know it.

The Critical Nib with Emma Lee
Editorial

The three reviews in this issue act as a reminder we very much live in a global village. Jacob Ross's thriller '*Black Rain* Falling' is set in the Caribbean but underlines the global nature of the drugs trade, a scourge to some but a needed income for others and the balancing act of policing. The police both need the cooperation of the people they police even when it conflicts with the need for natural justice. Nathaneal O'Reilly's *'(Un)belonging'* is a poetry collection from an Australian who has spent extended periods living in England, Ireland, Germany, Ukraine and the US, giving him a viewpoint from which to observe living patterns and behaviours from the vantage point of being an outsider. Mike Farren reviews Bhanu Kapil's *'How to Wash a Heart'* which explores rights and responsibilities between host and guest (in this case a refugee), the privileged and non-privileged, the default and other and the tensions that arise when the one cast in the role of guest behaves unconventionally or dares do something outside of the remit granted by the host.

Mike Farren is a new reviewer to The Blue Nib and one of several who responded to our recent recruitment drive. The Critical Nib has welcomed and looks forward to welcoming new reviews from Daniel Ajayi, Stephen A Allen, Jacqui Brown, Lynda Scott Araya, Justin Goodman, Phillip Hall, Chloe Jacques, Jagari Mukherjee, Charline Poirier, Declan Toohey plus a couple of others who have queried but not yet started reviewing. This is in addition to our regular team of James Fountain, Carla Scarano d'Antonio, Melissa Todd and Ada Wofford. We also still accepting submissions of unsolicited reviews. Please check out The Critical Nib on The Blue Nib's website which is updated with new reviews at least once a week.

Emma Lee
The Critical Nib Editor

Jacob Ross's *Black Rain Falling*,

'Black Rain Falling' Jacob Ross
Sphere
ISBN-13: 9780751574425
£14.99 (hardback)

Jacob Ross follows up 'The Bone Readers' which won the inaugural Jhalak Prize for Fiction in 2017, with 'Black Rain Falling'. Both work as stand alone novels set on the fictional Caribbean island of Camaho featuring Detective Constable and forensics expert Michael 'Digger' Digson.

The opening paragraph sets the scene, 'One think I learned from my two years fighting crime in Camaho – sometimes to uphold the law, you need to break the f--king rules.

'Five dates after I arrested a police officer for drink-driving and much worse, Miss Stanislaus, my partner in San Andrews CID, shot down Juba Hurst – the man who raped her as a child. The trouble I started was nothing compared to hers. And there was no way I was going to let her face the consequences on her own. That's me, Michael Digger Digson. It is the way I'm wired.'

This leaves Digger with two problems and a case. The case is a murder of a local man known to ship drugs. Miss Stanislaus is charged with murder, suspended from duty and given six days to clear her name. The drink-driving police officer ran over and killed a woman orphaning two young children, and, in Camaho not only is arresting a fellow officer seen as a transgression, it's punished no matter how serious the reason for arrest.

The punishment comes when the Justice Minister shuts down San Andrews CID where Digger works and splits the team, transferring Digger, along with his nominal boss Chief Officer Malan Greaves, to the station where the arrested police office worked.

Digger is allowed to continue working on the murder case, which triggers an investigation into Camaho's shadowy forests and well-connected drugs traffickers who, used to the police turning a blind eye, think they can ignore the law. The higher up the trafficking hierarchy, the less blatant the law-breaking is as transactions are covered by seemingly legitimate paperwork and businesses. Digger unofficially teams up with his police partner Miss Stanislaus, breaking back into the shut office, since the station he was transferred to isn't safe, where they're joined by their secretary and eventually Chief Officer Greaves, if only to keep an eye on Digger, since whatever Digger does will impact his career too.

Doing what he does best, Digger continues to dig. He discovers the villagers where the murdered man lived are fearful and reluctant to speak. Some of the young men, really still only teenagers, show whip scars. Rumours surface of a man called Shadowman. Through a student, Digger discovers there could be a potential drugs factory in the forests. The student is killed before Digger locates it. A colleague in narcotics confirms and estimates the scale of production. Together they figure out the size of boat required to ship the supply out. Digger uncovers links between Shadowman and Juba Hurst and begins to suspect that Shadowman isn't heading the operation. Someone far more powerful is. His investigation throws up more questions than answers, particularly when the criminals seem to be one step ahead of the police. When Miss Stanislaus queries the murdered man's mother as to where the money for her new electrical kitchen gadgets came from, she finds out the mother has been paid unofficial compensation and Digger follows the money trail.

Meanwhile he's not lost sight of the deadline in which to clear Miss Stanislaus' name. Digger isn't entirely without connections of his own, although the use of one might sacrifice his relationship with his girlfriend. He is not a reckless maverick, a one-man army against corruption, but a man whose respect has to be earnt and who will use his forensic knowledge and intelligent to solve a case and protect those he loves.

Miss Stanislaus is not a sidekick. Her skills, memory and ability to read people are skills that complement Digger's. Both value the spirit of the law, although not necessarily the letter, and neither have much time for politics. The interconnectedness of those in positions of power and familial links Digger uncovers are credible on a small island. In effect Camaho becomes just as much a character as the people. Transporting the plot to say London or Miami wouldn't work, which is why the location to 'Black Rain Falling' is so vital.

'Black Rain Falling' stands shoulder to shoulder with the prize-winning 'The Bone Readers' as masterclasses in crime novels where readers care as much about the detectives as the victims, where grief is raw and the characters are not mere pawns to show off the detectives' brilliance. The overall narrative arc builds towards a gripping climax – there are chapters where the reader will not want to put the novel down – but the subplots allow space for the reader to stop and absorb events, to see the sun glinting off a boat, feel the shadows in the forest, the torrential downpour and appreciate how smoothly the subplots are woven into the main plot and how police operate with the consent of those they serve and keeping the balance of conflicting interests is delicate, underappreciated skill.

Emma Lee

Bhanu Kapil's *How to Wash a Heart*

How To Wash a Heart **Bhanu Kapil**
Liverpool University Press
ISBN: 978-1-789-62168-6
£9.99 (hardback)

In an intense, wide-ranging exploration of relations between host and guest, this collection – Kapil's first to be published in the UK – presents within itself a kind of analogue for that relationship. There are elements it's easy to settle into – the regularity of the poems (all 20 to 23 lines) and the sections (all of eight pages); the mostly end-stopped lines which, taken individually, present clear, declarative thoughts. And yet, any notions of comfort are constantly undercut by tensions both in the narrative and in the sense at the level of individual lines and sentences.

To shed, briefly, my critical invisibility, one of the greatest tensions for me as a white, non-migrant reader was calibrating my own response and alignment. There are times – when the guest invites someone into her bedroom at night or leaves a wet towel on the bannister – that I felt myself sharing the host's exasperation that the guest dares to have her own life. And yet (that phrase again), this is a host who reads the guest's diary, frowns on friendship between the guest and her adopted daughter ('an "Asian refugee"') and ultimately [spoiler alert] betrays the guest. The negotiation of rights and responsibilities between host and guest / privileged and non-privileged / normative and 'other' is the central point here and it is (depending on one's perspective) refreshing, disturbing or both that the viewpoint is the one less commonly afforded a voice.

There is a strong sense from the beginning that the guest is in an impossible position. The second page begins with the assertion, 'I don't want to beautify our collective trauma' only for this to be modified within half a page –

'As a guest, I trained myself
To beautify
Our collective trauma.'

Victimhood and gratitude are performative: there is an expectation placed on the recipient of hospitality, though its opacity makes it difficult (or impossible) to negotiate:

'it's exhausting to be a guest
In somebody else's house
Forever.'

…because 'host logic / Is variable'.

While the relationship is established almost immediately, the guest's backstory emerges more slowly and in a more piecemeal fashion. In the first section, we learn only that she comes 'from a country / All lime-pink on the soggy map' and have to wait until the second section before an impressionistic personal history begins to emerge. However, even where the tone of these pieces begins in nostalgia, there is almost invariably an undermining note of violence. A reminiscence about a grandfather fermenting sweet yoghurt in the roots of a mango tree ends with the suggestion that those roots 'once concealed / A kill', while a story of a mother cooking okra is overwhelmed by a visceral sense of shame. Then, following a poem in which the narrator's home explodes, the hardships and humiliations of the migrant experience begin:

'The messages we received
Were as follows:
You are a sexual object, I have a right
To sexualize you.
You are not an individual.
You are here
For my entertainment.'

The host, however, attempts to draw a line under the guest's past, ending the third section's first poem with, 'I want to hear about what happened afterwards / Not before'. Sure enough, this is a section that contextualises the guest in her new reality. Days are counted off as she adapts to the host's household and art ('Was I your art?'). A visit from a cousin brings a shared reminiscence (about boring poetry) and 'reminds me / Who I really am' but the lessons learnt resolve to:

'The wealth and property
Of my host
Require constant surveillance.'

The final two sections complete the arc of what I had not realised on first reading is a heavily, if sometimes obliquely, narrative-driven work. In the fourth section, she ponders her own creativity, asking,

'Is a poet
An imperial dissident, or just

An outline
Of pale blue chalk?'

and elsewhere,

'How do you live when the link
Between creativity
And survival
Can't easily Be discerned?'

The fifth section accelerates through the breakdown in the façade of friendly relations, leading to the final betrayal.

The fourth section contains the second of two poems that begin by repeating the collection's title (though the collection's first poem could be seen as running on from the title). There's an additional 'How to wash a heart' poem in the 'Note on the Title' section at the end. While the function of the title in the main batch of poetry remains mysterious, this note locates its origin in a film, in which 'A heart appears in the air next to the body or bunched up on a T-shirt in the snow, in the film with Béatrice Dalle on the sleigh.'

This has clearly been an obsessive image for Kapil (urbandictionary.com has a 2008 definition of 'Heart' referencing this film from a contributor styled 'Bhanu: A Failed Novelist') but most significantly, it fed into 2019 performance of the same name. Again, though, the concept is elusive as Kapil notes, "In writing these new poems I diverged – almost instantly – from the memory of the performance." Instead, a voice – that of the guest – took over: fictional but drawing on Kapil's experiences of the limits of inclusivity in the '"mostly white" spaces' of American academia. In this context, does the written work's title have independent meaning (the uprootedness of the heart as in the Dalle-inspired image?) or does it simply sit under an umbrella title? This is one of the frustrations of the piece – that none but the few who saw the ICA performance will be able to trace links between the two.
'How to Wash a Heart' is uncomfortable and unclassifiable. However, as people seek, in these times, to calibrate and align in the light of Black Lives Matter, and as they perhaps feel trapped in the disrupted and unwelcoming space of their own COVID-besieged homes, it feels like an urgent and essential work.

Mike Farren

Nathaneal O'Reilly's *(Un)Belonging*

(Un)belonging Nathaneal O'Reilly
Recent Work Press
ISBN: 9780648685333 (paperback)

Nathaneal O'Reilly was born in Australia and has spent extended periods living in England, Ireland, Germany, Ukraine and the United States so is very familiar with being the outsider and attempts to belong. It's also a perfect viewpoint to observe and record those observations. The early poems mostly start in America, in 'Exploring the Neighborhood After Ten Days Confined at Home Due to Surgery'

'The woman with pink personalized
license plates proclaiming OIL WFE
is moving out, leaving trash behind.

The baseball fields, basketball
courts and playground are deserted,
kids trapped indoors by heat.

Old Ray on Olympic watches the street
on a white plastic chair in his open garage,
Katie panting faithfully by his side.

Empty recycling bins lie helpless
on their sides waiting for fathers
to come home and carry them inside.'

It brings to mind Georges Perec's 'Tentative d'épuisement d'un lieu parisien' (Attempt at exhausting a place in Paris) where the accumulative detail builds a picture of a place. Here suburban Texas, where the landscape defines the people. The woman with the 'pink personalised license plates' keeps her license plates so doesn't entirely leave all her trash behind. The residents dutifully take out their bins for emptying and, following convention, it's a man's job to bring them back in.

Two poems draw a compare and contrast between two presidents. 'The Boy from Hope' is Bill Clinton, whose childhood home is open to tourists,

'Still, one could imagine little Bill
tottering about on the front porch
taking the first steps towards

a remarkable career, watched casually
by his grandparents and widowed mother,
none of whom could possibly have imagined
what kind of man he would become—
brilliant, feared, admired, hated and flawed,
shades of Hamlet and Macbeth.'

Whereas a poem drawn from Trump's press conference on 16 February 2017, 'The Confessions of Donald J. Trump',

'President Putin called me up very nicely
to congratulate me on the win of the election.

I have nothing to do with Russia.
I told you, I have no deals there,
I have no anything.'

Whereas Clinton holds 'shades of Hamlet and Macbeth', Trump babbles to produce contradictory nonsense; hoisted by his own petard.

The collection moves on to recount a story from a great-uncle about the poet's great-great-grandfather who drowned in the Grand Canal in Dublin on a drunken walk home. The great-uncle finds it funny that a man of six foot three inches can drown in a canal that's five foot ten inches deep. When the poet visits the canal, he thinks he can take a short-cut by wading across it,

'into the muddy canal. I sank
to my right knee and panicked,
convinced another step forward
would suck me to the bottom.
Suddenly, a six-three drowning man
in a five-ten canal was no joke.'

The poet makes a hasty retreat. The second half of the collection moves back to Australia and family life. In 'Too Young' dedicated to the poet's daughter Celeste, she's 'too young to be embarrassed' by her father's antics, 'You joined in with the Maori kids,/ too young to know or care about race' and ends, 'You sipped lemonade, too young to understand/ why we cared about music from New Zealand'. The poem emphasises how prejudice is learnt, not innate and there's hope that children can also learn not to become prejudiced. Like the earlier Texan poems, these poems also allow cumulative details to tell a bigger story, in 'Refuge', an open field is tucked

'behind the strip mall
beside the medical center

a white-tail doe and her fawn
pause at the street's edge

before clicking across concrete
to the last stand of live oak'

'Beach Ballet' is a visit to Ireland where the poet is chatting to someone but looks towards the beach and sees a girl surfing,

'before stepping lightly off the side
of the board into knee-deep foam.
The girl's ride is almost complete

before I recognize her as my daughter,
just twenty minutes into her first lesson,
adapting, evolving, becoming herself.

Not recognising his daughter is a bonus, he gets to see her as if she were someone else's child developing skills and becoming independent. A loving parent's instinct is to protect and nurture but sometimes that conflicts with a child's growing independence and need to figure out how to do things for themselves. His daughter has benefited from the lack of parental interference.

Nathaneal O'Reilly has built a collection of gentle poems full of careful observations where readers are invited to picture the details and create the image and response requested in the poem. '(Un)belonging' explores the life of someone who is an outsider and the advantages of seeing the familiar through a different perspective.

Emma Lee

Seanchaí
Short Fiction

Haus des Meeres by Antony Osgood

On the second floor (Mediterranean & Tropical Fishes) Professor Frankl passes a guide politely explaining the history of the Aquarium to sceptical British tourists wearing baseball caps and sandals.

Frankl at this point usually begins to wonder if the steps go on forever. Will he *ever* reach the roof terrace? But today he feels there are insufficient steps. He coughs himself to business, makes a note to inform the guide his shirt should always be freshly pressed. He also writes: *All things end,* in a certain hand. The notebook and fountain pen find a perfect home in his jacket pocket: the line of material is undisturbed.

At the doorway to the third (Corals & Eels) Spanish tourists chewing gum feign interest in crocodiles whilst aching to discover the calibre of gun the Aquarium tower once boasted. How many flak-towers did Vienna boast? they demand to know, and answer, "Not enough!"

On this floor Frankl always suspects he is climbing a metaphor, and pauses for breath. This afternoon, an overwhelming urge to wash his hands engulfs him.

He stretches out his neck and steps on.

Arriving at the fourth (Café), Frankl listens to a harried young guide engage in confounding conversation with Americans concerning the construction of the tower, particularly whether prisoners of war (namely, *their* grandfathers) were used as slaves.

Here, Frankl often suspects he has climbed more steps than await him. He pushes through curtains of terminal desolation, as if walking on stage for a final bow. Today the fabric gathers about his feet.

"You must understand, all nationalities were prisoners *to* war," the guide explains. The Americans don't buy that. They believe war can be won easily as right can be made distinct from wrong. Frankl listens to the guide and nods; he makes a note to remind the guide of the protocols concerning permissible hair styles, and award her a commendation for bravery.

Pausing on the fourth, as if the sorrow of so few remaining steps is an anchor, Frankl busies himself with tidying his suit, employing fingers as disguise. He feels invaded, and not for the first time wishes this place didn't require tourists.

It is his belief that when visiting the city, guests speak as if only buildings matter. Frankl (who has been Director for twenty years) is principally enamoured with the archaeology of ideas, though he allows himself to appreciate that architecture is a canvas upon which humans paint the reinvention of themselves. It is the uses made of buildings that matter, Frankl often finds himself telling visitors.

Buildings, Frankl writes in his notebook, *are mirrors of dreams.*

Unusually, as if putting off the inevitable, he pauses at the Café long enough to take a macchiato. It is 'traversable' (meaning the coffee is a hard slog but passable). He smiles at his thin witticism and hands back the cup. He dabs his lips, feels for the notebook in his pocket, pats a tower wall.

Just as he turns to climb the steps, the florid Café manager calls his name (using an endearment!) and Frankl is handed complimentary cake. Frankl fails to hear apprehensive enquiries, and he barely examines the kuchen. This is so uncommon an event, the Café manager says later, alarm bells should have peeled across the whole of Vienna.

"Professor Frankl was always so precise in manners, clothes *and* cake!" the wailing manager will cry. "Polite to all staff. We were like *family.* His turning without thanks should have prompted me to tackle him to the floor!"
Frankl, had he known, might have said his staff were very much unlike his family. (Frankl preferred employees.)

*

He is breathless from melancholy; each step seems an angel wrestled. Frankl dislikes clichés as much as shirts not tailored but bought from a rack, but he might say, were he able to grant such soiled words entry to his lips (charging them an exorbitant admission), that he feels to be walking through a dream that's become a nightmare.

He sees reflected in a tank of piranha his own face lined with tears.

Still, up he climbs.

On the sixth floor (Chinese Salamanders) rather than face a press of Italian tourists, he pulls *punschglasur* from his coat. His eyebrows twitch in surprise at finding a poor rabbit in such a fine jacket, and he sighs. Bless the manager for his kind thought, but this cake is too sweet, too pale for his palate. A miserable nibble suffices to reveal the cake holds no artistry. Made by machine not hand, he'd wager. The new Director will be obliged to end the stocking of such unloved cake.

Frankl places the *punschglasur* in a bin so as not to make a mess, and wipes his mouth with a handkerchief. He pulls out his notebook, but doesn't know what to write, so returns it unopened to his pocket. This day as full of discontent, and blue unwritten words.

No further notes to the actors on this stage, he thinks.

He shakes himself. Opens the notebook as an excuse to catch his breath on the seventh (Gila Monster). He writes in walnut ink: *April 14th is too warm a day. The city's plush with people, bursting with life, and poor cake.*

The pen hovers, like a father not kissing a child for fear of waking it from dreams, until he can bear it no longer, and on a new page gently turned he writes: *To whom am I writing?*

Frankl lifts his fountain pen, sketches in the air an image of his Grandfather sitting atop the flak tower seventy-five years ago. He is watching Russian tanks crushing children as they skip home.

Another page, a second kiss: *We are curators of our history.*

The defeated man moves on, continues his painful ascent.

*

Yesterday afternoon, one month into his fitness routine, Frankl had been alarmed to discover the duration of his mid-afternoon climb *increasing*. The first peregrination from his ground floor office to the roof terrace had taken eight minutes and forty-three seconds, one step at a time. Yesterday, the climb required twenty-three minutes and sixteen seconds, *two* steps at a time.

He blamed Schultz. His Grandfather was also liable. But primarily he accused the sharks. Frankl often finds himself staring at the tenth-floor hammerheads (and Toilets). Yesterday he recognised predation in their eyes. He felt unable to escape.

The Amazonian rainforest on the ninth holds its temptations (not paying attention here *invariably* results in the damned monkeys stealing his glasses), but he knows they cannot hold him. The hammerheads, always calling, capturing his thoughts with their beauty, side-line feet, fill his lungs with seawater. The creatures should never have been thought of as suitable for his Aquarium, though the tourists love them, and the city desires a tourist's purse.

Yesterday, Frankl felt he'd been holding his breath whilst staring at the sharks.

For twenty years he's been treading water, predator-blind.

*

Today, the hammerheads seem neutral in their regard of him.

Sharks prefer live prey, not dead meat, he writes.

At the roof terrace Frankl inhales his beloved Vienna. He caresses the terrace mesh and surveys Esterházypark below. Café Ritter on nearby Mariahilfer Straße has served the finest *sachertorte* since 1867. Yesterday morning, immediately following Schultz's heroic leap from the roof terrace, Frankl had turned to his pale assistant and therefore naturally said, "Today, Maria, is a two slice *sachertorte* day. Ensure the cream is freshly whipped."

Admiring his city, Frankl imagines *that* is what the mayor took exception to. His otherwise exemplary actions following Schultz's unexpected swan dive were marred by the ordering of cake.

"You called for *sachertorte* before calling the *ambulance*?"

Frankl suggested an ambulance would provide little help, and what is an emergency without a little sweetness to see one through?

"You should have phoned for *shovels*," the mayor shouted.

Staring toward the MuseumsQuartier, Frankl writes in his notebook. *History, like the eyes of a hammerhead, has keen depth of vision; once it spots you, escape is not permitted.*

Sun through sticky eyelashes crafts rainbows in his eyes. He touches the concrete of the tower, as if comforting a pleasing dog. He touches the mesh where Schultz had climbed; eyes follow the distortion caused by boots. The crate of beer, upon which his Grandfather stood to launch Schultz up and over the mesh, has yet to be seized by the Police. Frankl takes a beer, pops the stopper and doesn't rest until the bottle is empty. He turns a new page. There are so few remaining.

Being childless, I write to the city.

*

For the last two decades the group of elderly men have appeared, demanding discounted entry every 13th April. Led by Frankl's own Grandfather, the troop insist on reparations, namely, the best seats on the terrace, an eye turned the other way, and free coffee. Over the years their numbers diminish, but the gang become *louder* the more their hearing fails, they dance for longer the more arthritis grinds their bones, beyond raucous as their ranks reduce and schadenfreude engulfs them.

The irregular remnants of the 2nd Panzer Corps of the Sixth Panzer Army sashay grandly about the terrace, toss off sketches, toast their beautiful defeat at the hands of Szokoll's Austrian Resistance Group and the Soviet 46th Army. They smuggle their own alcohol into the Aquarium and delight tourists.

Are all families part circus? he writes.

In 1945, the city defenders had been doomed to fail. They suspected their true mission was not to protect the streets but the idea of a lost Vienna. The 2nd Panzer Corps had long ago mislaid their tanks but not their schnapps or vodka, and their backpacks were crammed with solen paint and brushes. For every pistol, they carried three canvases. They possessed more easels than helmets, felt safer for it. The Corps took a vote and agreed they required not bullets but perspective, and pausing on their way only to bake *sachertorte* in the kitchen of Café Ritter, they liberated the flak tower, enjoying a swig of cooking sherry on each floor. On the roof terrace white bed sheets painted with sketches and encouraging messages in Russian were waved, photographs of one another were taken, and a gramophone discovered. They danced while they painted the end of the world. It wasn't long before everyone on the ground began to shoot at the pirouetting child soldiers on the roof. No side welcomed jeering kids. Their war was a serious matter, not suitable for art on bed sheets.

Frankl's Grandfather led the Corps. He was at that time busy pretending not to be Jewish. He camouflaged himself in plain sight by dint of a good Austrian name, assuaged guilt by hiding bullets in bidets and encouraging artistic revolution among the tankless soldiers. Grandfather saved all his Corps but one, the youngest. Atop the flak tower that day little Max turned eight. He fell without making a sound, his easel flapping behind him as if it were a parakeet. Max died a victim of mistimed steps, art, and schnapps.

"He *flew* from us!" Frankl remembers Grandfather saying.

Both Germans and Russians shot Max as he fell. The Austrian Resistance Group removed their hats in respect; they cried as the child fell. He seemed lighter than air, swooped like a feather. They beckoned him toward their waiting arms. Max missed joining the resistance, and the resistance could not catch Max.

War is a cloth bag, Frankl writes, *full of tears and outstretched hands, stitched by missed opportunities to be kind.*

That most of the Corps survived was worth an anniversary drink.

Frankl never objected to their singing, nor their ironic saluting. He did not even mind their habit of achieving inebriated enlightenment by eleven in the morning. Yesterday, it wasn't their drinking that caused an impact, but the falling.

Having spent a whole life climbing, there is grandeur in falling from great heights, Frankl writes, admiring, through prism eyes, Vienna.

His heart calms. He is recovered from his ascent.

*

Being a responsible man (unlike Grandfather) Frankl asked Maria to fetch the insurance documentation after the cake. Being Director obliged him to consider not the horror of a falling veteran but practicalities. Frankl dared not contemplate what the events meant for him personally, because he immediately knew.

"You checked paperwork before seeing the *damage* that old fucker caused?" the mayor asked. "Did you hide away, eating cake, reading cowardly documents, all the time expecting *more* veterans to fall from the sky?"

"For three generations my family has overseen the conversion of the flak tower into a tourist attraction, sir," Frankl had said, and was told to be hushed. He knew at that moment – with that dismissive hush - his future, proficiently as he did his history, as he knew each step, each exhibit, each story the tower contained. Where shells were once piled, there now was ocean life. And where there once stood a Frankl, guiding the tower toward peaceful dreams, there stood a conservative mayor.

He thinks of his Grandfather, always resisting. Standing on a crate of beer, Frankl believes seventy-five years is nothing to history, and that this city will always be keen to seize any excuse to rid itself of an upstart Jew. He writes, as if he is a Hofburg on a horse: *Grandfather is a family curse of a hero, too precious to be hidden.*

That ex-Private Schultz leapt from the terrace and fell upon a group of tourists, killing two and causing trauma to dozens, was disquieting enough. (Frankl knows Schultz landed so hard that for the whole of the forthcoming tourist season the wide outline of liquefied *once*-Private Schultz's body will be visible.) What *rankled* the mayor was that Schultz had inadvertently landed on Israelis. And so publicly! The mayor was voted in because of his hatred of minorities, but such an obvious action was not his style at all.

"It looks like a *racist* suicide!" the mayor claimed.

For Frankl, like his Grandfather, the anti-Semitism stitched into the history of Vienna is often far less overt than Schultz's fall. He feels it under his nails. He smells it on street corners, in the grind of every coffee.

"Such catastrophic synchronicity!" the mayor complained. A delegation needs to visit Tel Aviv to apologise, Frankl was informed. (And spend a few days sightseeing, paddling, eating out, all at the city's expense, Frankl *didn't* say.) That the falling ex-child soldier was a painter, a pacifist, a hater of Nazis, an artist whose work pursued yellow stars at night on canvas, made little difference.

Friendly fire, Frankl writes, *remains fire.*

Frankl has no idea what possessed Schultz to choose the seventy-fifth anniversary of the fall of Vienna to kill himself. What is certain is that Schultz had been helped over the mesh barrier. (Only a rare eighty-eight-year-old might be so independently athletic.) Frankl knew his Grandfather had given Schultz a bunk-up.

Grandfather, being the oldest of the child soldiers, their commander, had ordered his Corps to climb the flak tower, and then to descend like hell when everyone shot at them. It was Grandfather who gathered Max's broken body, Grandfather who with bleeding hands had buried Max in buckets among the debris of a fallen city. It is *always* Grandfather. Even the Aquarium was his idea.

"He *flew* from us, too!" Grandfather had cried yesterday. "Another little boy!"

"He was eighty-eight and–"

"Artists can never afford to grow old!"

He was weeping, laughing between tears, holding tightly to his Grandson, staining with dust-tears Frankl's new jacket. They held one another. Words failed them.

You never let go of Grandfathers. They are your history. They held you, then you hold them.

*

Forty-seven metres takes so little time to fall.

Schultz was probably unable to complete the melody he was singing. Frankl wonders whether Schultz hoped to fly twice around the tower just to finish the song. Had Schultz flown, Frankl imagines the ghost of an anti-aircraft weapon would appear, shooting viscous shells at the singing veteran. Because anything is possible. Except acceptance.

Frankl strokes the mesh of the roof terrace, and he knows just what can be achieved if belief is written a blank cheque. It can buy a flak tower and transform it into an Aquarium. It allows boys who are old men to fly. It motivates a Grandfather to pass on a dream.

But for how long might belief survive life?

*

The mayor, that writer of city cheques, that popularist *canceller* of budgets, called the Aquarium this morning. Frankl must resign. Given his family's history, he has no choice.

Haus des Meere will be someone else's dream.

Frankl stares across dry-eyed Vienna. With any luck, *he* might land upon his meddlesome Grandfather, *relatively* friendly fire remaining fire. Frankl straddles the mesh as if sitting atop a beautiful hammerhead. He writes: *History causes some to fall to ruin, some to hide. Others transform into a home for sharks.*

Professor Frankl stretches one leg into the Viennese afternoon, and lets it hang.

Writing is a wish to be remembered, if only as a fool who cannot spell, he scribbles.

He turns a page against the wind and stares across red roofs. Vienna is crammed and it is empty. He examines his notebook. Each entry less neat than the last, as if climbing into the sky has starved him of oxygen. And so? Each word, no matter how deformed, tells of his existence.

He stares at the final page of his notebook. He cannot see for sparkle.

Given Austria's history, Frankl writes, *perhaps we should all resign.*

He rips out white pages, tosses them as if gifting the wind. Confetti-words fall childless. Tears in his eyes cause Vienna to fracture. He steps toward his beloved city, and begins to sing.

Carousel by Helen Campbell

"Terrible shame about Marianne," my mother says out of the blue.

"What do you mean?" I'm preoccupied, rooting in her wardrobe. Among the clothes on the shelf, I'm trying to find something that actually belongs to her. I wonder where the blue cashmere cardigan I gave her for Christmas is gone.

"Dead!" The word shoots across the room. She is quite emphatic, sitting rigidly straight, smoothing flat the top sheet on the bed, fingers spread, daring it to crinkle up again. "Suddenly, no warning. Just gone."

"Who told you that, Mam?"

"Oh, for goodness sake, everybody knows. Sure even you must have heard about it. Mind you," she's on a roll now, "she wasn't that easy to get on with, you know. I haven't seen her in ages. We had a big row. Can't remember for the life of me what it was about."

I remember what it was about. Me bringing her to this place.

"Well, you know what I always say - what goes round, comes round." She sniffs her all-knowing sniff.

"Yes, Mam, that's what you always say." I determine to be reasonable, a triumph of wishful thinking over experience. I sit down on the edge of her bed, carefully modulating my voice.

"If you mean me, Mam, I'm not dead. I'm here."

My mother looks at me for a long moment. Her eyes narrow with suspicion.

"Don't be ridiculous, of course I don't mean you. I'm talking about Marianne, my daughter. How could I mean you?"

Indeed, how could she mean me, Marianne, her daughter? Apart from the odd moment of lucidity, she hasn't known me for a long time. In spite of my resolutions, I feel my shoulders tensing up.

"So, who do you think I am then?" I almost shout, till I remember where we are.

However, she decides that the subject is closed. She moves on.

"I need to go to the toilet."

"Okay, hang on; I'll call a nurse."

"Can't you bring me?"

"No!" I sound too loud. "I'd better call a nurse - I'd be afraid I might let you fall."

I practically run for the door, pouncing on a nurse hurrying down the corridor. She comes at once, her upbeat tone having none of the underlying desperation I detect in my own voice. Sometimes I'd give my right arm to be able to cajole people to do things they don't want to do.

While they adjourn to the bathroom, I stand by the window, leaning my forehead against the cool glass. The attempt at a Zen garden outside is obviously intended to induce calm; but to me the few scrawny conifers struggling to survive among the pale stones reinforce the bleakness I feel. I check my watch, only forty minutes before I can reasonably say I have to dash home to the kids.

All too soon they are back; the nurse gently helps Mam into the bed, smiling at her as she checks that the top sheet is straight.

"Your mother is a real lady." Her voice tinkles like glass, her Filipino accent clear as crystal. "She likes things just so."

She smooths down my mother's hair. "You should spend more time sitting out with everyone else, Margaret. It's not good for you to spend all day in bed."

"I prefer my own company, thank you."

The nurse turns to me. "Maybe you could persuade Margaret to join in some of our activities. We have a lot of things going on." I smile ruefully at her. Full marks for trying.

My mother sinks back on the pillow as the nurse leaves the room. Suddenly, she opens her eyes wide. "I don't like it here. It's not a nice place."

"Oh Mam, it's lovely. You're always saying the food is delicious." A slight exaggeration on my part.

"It's not the food – it's the people." Clutching at the bed covers, she pulls herself forward to whisper.

"They're all having sex!"

Jesus, I suppress a snort - of laughter or hysteria, I'm not sure. Sex was not a word we were ever permitted to utter in our house.

"What are you talking about, Mam?" I try to sound serene, keep my voice even.

"I'm telling you, that bitch in reception is having sex with all the men."

"Ah, Mam, come on, you're making this up." Now I am shocked.

"Don't be ridiculous, don't I hear them at it all night." She's becoming very agitated. "It's disgusting."

I'd have to agree with her there. The 'bitch' in reception is the glamorous owner of the nursing home, a highly organised woman. She churns out instructions and accounts with the same ruthless efficiency. While they advertise person centred care, somehow I doubt that it stretches this far.

"So can I go home now? I can't stand it any longer."

We are back on familiar turf again.

"The doctor says it's too soon, Mam. A few more weeks."

"Sure he's been saying that for months." She insists. "The grass must need cutting by now. And the poor cat, she'll be wondering if I'm ever coming come back."

"The cat is fine, Mam. We feed her every day." How easily the lie slips out. The poor cat has long gone to meet its maker under the wheels of a neighbour's car.

"Do you know what, Mam – I think it's high time we did your nails?"

It works. It always works.

"Oh that would be nice." She sits back against the pillow; a faint smile lifts her face.

"You remember the article in your magazine, Mam, with all the instructions?"

"Course I do."

That's good. It was a long time ago; I was still a teenager when the article caught our fancy for some reason. Doing our nails became a ritual between us. Now, it's the only personal service I can willingly do for her, the only pleasurable activity we share.

She stretches out her hands obediently. No rings, they have long gone missing as she shuttled back and forth between care homes and hospitals. Despite the deep blue veins and the liver spots, her hands are still beautiful, the fingers long and tapered. The nails unbitten. Nail-biting was high on the list of deadly sins in our family. And the list was a lot longer than seven.

On the bedside table, I set out the tools of the trade, in strict order, the nail polish standing proud at the end of the line. 'Carousel' in bright letters on the label. I switch my phone to silent – previous experience having indicated that it doesn't do to be interrupted while wielding a brush dripping with rose red nail polish. Her eyes follow me as I fill the bowl with warm water from the hand basin and place it on the tray. Turning up the sleeves of her bed jacket, we embark on the ceremony.

First, taking each finger at a time, I file the nails to a neat oval shape. Neatness was one of the most prized attributes in my mother's esteem. Poor grooming was generally regarded as a sign of moral decay. After that, a gentle rubbing in of exfoliator. According to the article, which I still remember word for word, 'the removal of dead cells is a prerequisite to healthy skin'. My mother's hands feel like small birds, filaments of bone barely held together with skin so transparent you can almost see right through it. It's as if you only had to squeeze lightly to crush her hands into fragments. Then I place both hands into the warm water for the exfoliator to do its work. She doesn't stir. I check my watch – time matters in these instances. According to the instructions - between five and ten minutes is optimal. I softly swish the water round the bowl. These are the hands that sewed my clothes, baked the cakes, sorted the laundry, administered the odd slap for long forgotten crimes. I find myself in danger of becoming maudlin, so I hurry on the process.

I pat her hands dry with the soft towel I brought, rub in some cuticle cream then begin to massage her hands and arms with lavender scented hand cream. As our fingers meld together in the fragrance, I realise how rarely we have ever held hands.

Mortified, I recall the awkward hug I tried to give her when I first brought her here a year ago. She pulled away from me, well aware of my treachery. Anyway, we were never a touchy-feely family.

I gently push back the cuticles with the orange stick then go over each nail with cotton wool dipped in varnish remover to prepare for the final application.

"Nearly there now, Mam."

But she knows that and keeps her eyes closed. I often wonder where she goes in that dreamy state. I hope it's a good place. I spread the towel under her hands. With great care, I lift each finger and brush on the base coat. She opens her eyes and glances down. She nods to herself, satisfied that I am performing the task properly.

Reverently, I unscrew the top of the nail polish bottle. I always use Carousel. Dipping in the brush, tapping it on the edge of the bottle, I carefully draw the rosy red polish down each nail - cotton bud at the ready in case I stray onto the skin. Mam doesn't move a muscle. By the time I have finished both hands, the first nails are almost dry. Now it only remains to apply the top coat.

"Now for a long-lasting shine," I say, as always. We smile at each other in complicity, whisked back for an instant to another era, when we played out different roles.

"You have lovely hands Mam."

"You got my long fingers, you know."

I'm caught off guard. I reach out my hands and our fingers touch. She's right. I have inherited her long fingers and a lot of other qualities I'd find it hard to acknowledge. I see time passing across our hands. For a brief moment, I recognise the person I used to know. And I catch a glimpse of the person I am becoming.

A nurse appears with a tea tray. I pour the tea; Mam waves her fingers in front of her, blowing on them to make sure they are dry. We drink our tea and she nibbles a bourbon cream. The others she asks me to pop into her handbag for later. To join the rest of the crumbs residing there.

Surreptitiously I begin to gather my things together to leave, hoping she won't notice. She does.

"Sure you've only just arrived."

"Mam, I have to get back to sort out dinner for the kids."

"How are they? It's been ages since I saw them."

I can't explain to her that I prefer to visit her on my own. Totally unreasonable, I know. But I can't bear anyone else to witness the sort of person I am with my mother. And the betrayal I see in her eyes each time I say goodbye. And the tears of guilt I shed in the car on the way home.

"They're busy studying for their exams."

"I'll say a prayer for them. And sure I'll be ready to go back with you next week."

"We'll see, Mam." I pull on my jacket.

She studies her hands again. "Why did you change the colour?"

"I didn't – it's the same colour we always use – Carousel."

"No, this is definitely much brighter. It's too pink." She purses her lips. "I think it looks a bit common." Being common was the worst sin of all.

"Oh, for God's sake, Mam, you're never happy with anything I do."

"Don't be ridiculous, I only said I prefer the other colour."

"What other colour?"

And we're off again, on the eternal merry go round.

Jumpers by Delia Pring

I can either keep quietly screaming through life, or accept that *this life* is not right for me. It's the choice I must make. To either struggle with the pandemonium or take some time to look at the sky before silence. It's like the falling man.

*

The Gallery

Breathing deeply, I caress the dense material sitting inert upon the benchtop. Waiting to be manipulated, forced into twisted positions, exaggerated curves and indents. A performance of static movement.

I'm comfortable within these rooms when the gallery is closed. Here I escape from expectations, there's freedom to create. I work alone, unwilling to share this time. The hours before opening where I can focus on personal projects. Not that the mainstay of the gallery isn't enjoyable. The satisfaction of throwing a vase, the hypnotic motion of the wheel and the pleasure of packaging the piece up after purchase. It was bread and butter work, generic for the paying customers, it kept the gallery open. The evening workshops allow some space for innovation; teaching others the joy of craft and creation. But this pales in comparison with my private projects. Pouring forth twisted forms: limbs, torsos, faceless, erratic, partial people distorted in their familiarity. Grotesques. 'They remind me of Dante,' someone once said, 'or Blake.'

The encrusted overall is shrugged on eagerly. The delicate prints that make up my public uniform eclipsed. Now I'm imagination's slave, a bold confident creator, passionate in my ideas and the ambition to exhibit a full collection. Nightmares are my friends, waking me so I can seek solace with work, the scent of damp clay under my fingernails.

Insomnia has its advantages as the sun tentatively breaks through the trees, introducing a new day with optimism and coffee. As the dawn advances, I work vigorously, capturing the frenzied inspiration which hits as the pressure of opening hours creeps closer. Here time is fleeting, scrabbled together before customers and routine.

A retro bell and hammer clock jumps across the parquet floor. I must tear myself away to silence it. Drifting from my work, I shed the overall, stepping fluidly from it. Turn the clock off, give it three winds and replace it on the desk. Wash hands and face, apply subtle make up in the tiny toilet. Draw shoulders back, fix the public smile to this face. Another day.

*

What will it feel like?

Calm hopefully.

Is it like dreaming? I hope to have one good dream. When everything just feels right.

There's only one way to know.

Today?

It's as good as any. Are you ready?

Of course. I can't do anything spontaneous.

She stares at the photograph on the fridge held in place with a brightly coloured magnet.

Why him?

Because he is perfect.

What makes him perfect? It's not like you knew him.

It's because nobody and everybody knows him. Someone loved him, someone misses him. But no one wants him. In this instant, he is everything anybody can be.

I don't understand you on this.

He is the perfect paradox. Neither dead or alive. The Schrodinger's cat of our time. Strong yet vulnerable. Wild but controlled. He made a choice of how to be remembered and how to live. You're drawn to look, but you know you shouldn't, almost guilt in the fascination. You shouldn't find any beauty in such violence.

You really think about this, don't you?

He made a choice where there wasn't one.

I touch the faded clipping. 'The Falling Man' by Richard Drew.

There were so many of them. So many. And nobody wanted them to be seen, like they didn't exist because then it's all too real.

I don't exist.

Censored away. But they should have been celebrated because they made their choice. To have that one last look at the sky. It must have been like flying. And they were destroyed, you know. On impact. They hit the ground so hard.

This has nothing to do with us.

Taking the photograph, I pad to the bathroom and begin to run the taps. Light candles, add bubbles. The window is wide open.

Every time I think I can't keep going, he helps me make a choice, because even though he had limited options, he had the ability to own his choice in the end. We all need to own our choices.

The water helps me relax, enveloped by scent and softness. I look at the picture blu-tacked to the tiles at the foot of the bath. The choice where there was none and the dignity gained by it being made.

You're really doing this?

They will figure out why.

This doesn't feel like flying.

*

The Gallery

On the counter, I keep a book. Inside are all my creations, documented, named, numbered. They are individuals. If they get lost I can claim them. I know who they were.

*

Home

I wander through the house with the picture-perfect rooms, the careful façade which greets the weekly book club, this staged normality. The lounge, rarely used, is passed by. I close the door.

What do they think when they see me?

They think you're insane.

I sit on the worktop and inhale the room. Pale yellow walls with blue gloss. It shouldn't work, but it does. A leap of faith in B&Q with a clipping from a Sunday magazine. Well-worn units, solid pine (obviously) carefully painted cream and then sanded back allowing the wood to peek through. Mismatching ceramic knobs adorn the doors, all from different markets, shops, countries, eBay (but don't tell anybody). An open plate rack is above the toaster; a large wooden chopping board still has this morning's crumbs. In the plate rack is an assortment of dishes, bits of many sets that have dwindled, but still function. Breakfast dishes drain by the sink that is in front of the window. A ceramic jar, made to look like celery holds the dish brush and brillo pads. In the alcove is the Aga. Comforting and warm, the enamel kettle waits on the lid, oven gloves draped over the bright stainless-steel rail. There are biscuits in a Quality Street tin, and utensils hanging from a set of hooks. There is a table with four chairs, it extends but hasn't for a long time. There are books on the table with corners folded and notebooks and a bunch of pens and pencils in a jar. An aging spaniel used to nestle in the armchair: still covered with a crochet blanket, just in case he was damp from his dewy morning waddle round the lawn.

This is a space that has taken time to cultivate, time to collect and wear the edges away. Soft and simple, with the smell of toast and marmite, instant coffee. My utopia.

The bath is running; I planned this, to prove it is not a spontaneous reaction.

You don't do spontaneous.

This is my decision.

It's not one of your best

I'm sick of the sessions, her sycophantic voice, the bit of lipstick on her teeth… why is there always lipstick on her teeth? Does the woman get ready in the dark?

Stop going, don't take the meds, don't look at her bloody teeth.

*

#29 Luke

He doesn't want to be born this one. The clay detaching from the frame with satisfying dense thuds. I try to mould it back, vainly willing him to hold together. The twisted torso and far flung arms, defying gravity, succumbing to the weight.

"Please stay together, stay with me."

Determination overrides practicality as I force material onto the unstable structure. He responds, discarding extremities. I throw myself around his body, fingers splayed willing him to stay, my hair creates another texture upon his skin. This is the closest I have come to a hug for months.

How long is he going to take? He looks like shit.

I'm not giving up on this one. He's in here, I just need to get him out.

Are you the best person to do that?

I'm the only one that can.

You look like shit.

As the clay dries into my clothes, I scrape my hair back into an elastic band. Nine days I have been with him; he has caused me little sleep, heated arguments and reconciliations. I stink, sweat, cigarettes, cold coffee. I lean into him, and rest my cheek against the smooth surface of his back. His head lolls sideways away from me, slides forward and hits the floor with an explosive sickening thud. Instinctively I throw myself towards it, but it's beyond saving. As his eyes turn towards mine, angry sobs hurt my throat and bubble from my lungs, snot floods my nostrils. I am not an attractive crier. I hit him, again and again tearing his body apart with broken fingers. Later I wake up on the floor alone.

I told you he was shit.

*

Appointment 5

'Yes, I am here to see Dr Morris, 11:45.'

These places make me nervous. Absentmindedly I scroll through my phone, trying to look busy, like this is an everyday occurrence. Trying to appease that relentless inner voice that demands answers.

I promise that I won't let them take you. They can't make you leave anyway. You're here because I need you. You said it was a good idea. To get help. You look after me and in turn I will not let them take you. No, I promise it will go back to normal afterwards, it will be safe again, but something needs to change. Everything will be fine. I promise.

'Please come in, take a seat. Do you want a drink?'

Say no, you're fine. You've got one already.

'I got a coffee on the way.'

Sit up, look like you're fine. Make eye contact, answer like we practised,

then we can go.

'So, we left it last time with looking at breaking habits. You show signs of 'ritualistic behaviours' '

'It's more organised than 'ritualistic'; routine, then nothing gets disturbed and then I am left alone. It's best to stick with what you know, to stay safe.'

Look at her. She knows I'm here.

'Safe from what? Do you feel threatened?'

That's a leading question. They're not allowed to ask leading questions. I told you this would happen.

'No! it's to stop things going wrong, to stay controlled. But then again, I have been told to try everything once, else you might never know you like it.'

Where did that little anecdote come from? Who told you this?

'Sorry, that was a tangent.'

I sip at my coffee, distracting myself.

People like this are clever, they find ways to get things from you, for you to let go of your deepest secrets, and then I'll be gone and where will you be? Who will keep you safe?

'What sort of things would you try?'

'I don't think about it. It's best to stay with what you know. There can be no surprises then,

or disappointments.

I am not pathetic; I'm needed to be'

'Sorry, I don't understand.'

'I can do more, I want to do more, but

may I suggest you leave now

it's difficult. I know I'm safe where I am.

may I suggest you stop talking

I mean it's not much to ask from me really. It has got me through so much.

shut the hell up

But then again, I never know what to do, I'm always aware there is more, that there can be more to this but the risks'

…you're fucked

'Do you want to discuss this? We can arrange another appointment.'

I am not ignorant of the joy in her mind.

*

#11 Alayne.

She came out easily. Pliable, graceful, tall and smooth. Like a dancer stretching on tiptoes. Toned, athletic. Everything I'm not. No hint of trauma, no sweat, blood or tears. Claimed and awaiting collection. She never even went on display.

You don't like her, do you?

No, I fucking hate her.

*

Appointment 1

These rooms are designed to make you feel comfortable, apparently; I find nothing comfortable about a Formica table and wipe clean chairs, must just be me. The reassuringly bespectacled creature opposite, knees crossed, clipboard with my pile of notes. I know what they contain.

Overdose aged 20, ketamine.

Overdose age 15, miscellaneous tablets.

Signs of split personality.

Irrational repetitive behaviours.

Possible PTSD.

Obsessive.

Recurrent hallucinations

Historical eating disorders

It's endearing really to be broken down to these elements. Neutral coloured pen at the ready. Give it a minute. There will be the assurances of confidentiality, nothing leaves this room. I know this, but the thing is that I can't ever escape, that it will always know, will punish me for any little mistake. So far, we have skirted round and round. Yes, I had a perfectly normal upbringing,

No daddy issues, did well in school, cut yourself in the toilets on lunchbreak one Tuesday.

No, I wasn't hugely popular, but I didn't mind. Yes, I did ok at uni.

Stay forgettable, don't get involved, people are only there to hurt you.

I acknowledge I had a problem. I don't feel like I have had the best career, but I am fulfilled with what I do. Yes, I run a shop, well it's all unique pottery, local artists, some of my own work.

Do you still have those scars…?

So, I spew forth my uneventful life, the normality, the resignation to it. That I have ritualistic behaviour because I am pathetically dull.

Pathetic, alone, and mine.

We talk with stunted politeness, this is a waste of NHS funding; she is persistent, hoping there will be a breakthrough that will prove this is her vocation.

*

#32 Jonathan

He held together, perfect as he went for firing. It's up to him now, I've done all I can. Like a butterfly emerging from a chrysalis I wait with building anticipation. His ancestors lie in the reclaim bin, the next generation awaits in my mind.

Today I showered, washed and plaited my hair, all clean clothes. The shop is swept, cleaned and ready. Displays of the new glazed housewares are lit. I have made a space, not conspicuously for his arrival. It's a special day.

Wait 'til later.

No, he is going to be perfect. I know what I was doing wrong. He is ready.

I excitedly open the door, throwing it wide. And pieces start to fall, making beautiful music as they hit the floor. Details I had lovingly crafted pouring to my feet, a finger, nipple, unblinking eye. I wipe away silent tears, and go back into the brightly-lit gallery. Fix my smile and turn the sign to open.

*

Therapist Supervision

She was always cautious. So complex, but you couldn't help liking her; she needed a friend. I think I was the closest she ever got. She seemed under control, aware of keeping up the persona. But I agree she was afraid of something. The voice in her head; Wendy. Or maybe its silence. I was never sure. She kept explaining about this epiphany, that she could make 'the choice'. There was nothing religious about her, I asked her if it was connected to religion and she laughed at the absurdity. 'Nobody is that crazy'. She said; 'Nobody is that crazy'. She could escape in her work, get lost. This meant she would disappear, for extended periods. I assume this was when she was in the throes of mania. The rest of the time she seemed desperately sad. Sad and lonely. The creation of herself she described as 'a shroud she willingly wove and wore.' Wendy helped her; kept her controlled. She would work frantically. I could tell if she had been working, or was near to working. It went in waves. She would come back thin and pale, but animated, nervous energy. Her hands wouldn't stop and her eyes would bore into me, trying to make me understand. Obsessive? Very. Especially about Wendy. She would have full conversations. Wendy gave her the confidence to fly, to make choices, her guidance, protection, but also her demon, a parasite. She was always watching. Wendy was destructive; we were working towards breaking free from her. To stop the cycle of her control. She said once, 'She chips away, and I listen and act. I fall to pieces then try to rebuild myself. But each time I lose more little pieces, slivers seem to disappear and I am less and less.' I thought it was beautiful. The falling man? He was a symbol for 'the choice'. In the way she wanted to live, I think, or die.

*

Home

She closed the door on her neatly ordered home. Pressed her forehead to the sanded pine, took in a deep breath and turned around, eyes tightly closed.

Here was her secret. Where people never came, that nobody ever saw. This is not who she was, rather what she had been made to be. How she coped with the façade of 'normality', or the turmoil of the battles within herself. Hidden behind a flimsy barrier, this is where it got to her; this is where she didn't control, no matter how she tried to organise, tidy, make things liveable, extend the fantasy of the chocolate box life she craved and formulaically created.

A naked light bulb illuminated the detritus of her mind, chaos building in layers from the small patch of cream carpet where she stood, staggering upwards, gripping the walls, balancing ever more unstable, a loose grip on a weak foundation. Clothing spilled out from a dark wood chest of drawers, a pair of doors disembowelling itself, spewing forth floral prints, dark jeans, coloured scarfs, the uniform in which she faces the world. All of it is clean. She does not allow the dirt which fills her mind to infiltrate any part of the house, even here. It all starts folded neatly in the basket, fresh from the laundry room, where the clothesline levitates it above the threadbare tasselled rug, the pattern indiscriminate after thousands of footsteps. Here the windows are always open to let in the breeze, gently pushing the scented fabric conditioner aroma into the house where it can mingle with lavender candles, warm incense and the slight tang of wet spaniel. But once it comes through this door, as everything else, it descends to chaos. Here it doesn't seem to matter, here nothing has a place, what is the point?

The window is closed; to keep bedlam in. The curtains are open but loose from their matching tie backs which hang forgotten. She can see the stars on a clear night, awake and staring into the blackness that engulfs her. She doesn't like to sleep here. This is when she is vulnerable, anxious and afraid. This is where she is not herself, or is this where she is most herself? Here she lies awake in the tangled plethora of bedding wondering, questioning, waiting for the replies that will surely come through. This is the space she owns that in turn owns her. This is the space that allows her to not function whist in the throes of mania.

As she pads forward, books creak underfoot, half-forgotten jumpers, newspaper articles and hastily-sketched images struggle for attention and receive none. She surveys the bed. The patchwork cover, multiple blankets of varying size and texture, a heavy feather duvet with its matching pillows crumpled in the aftermath of another nightmare.

Her skin shines like a pearl, bright and smooth under the artificial glare of the bulb. She arches her back and moves her shoulders, trying to wriggle the day out of her muscles. They relax and with that she withers, the weight of effort too much to bear. Exhausted and unshielded, she finds an open wound in the beast of her cradle and inserts her body slowly, not wanting to disturb its weighty slumber, backing into the obscure recesses where she could maybe be unnoticed tonight. She extends a hand and pulls the beaded cord eradicating the luminosity highlighting her weakness. She hides in the dark, eyes wide waiting to see if it will come tonight or allow her some relief.

*

#45 Danny

How can you do this to me? Look at the state of you. You need me, but here you are all *'free'*, *'independent'*. How free do you feel? You can't survive without me. You don't eat, smoke, bathe. You're encrusted with filth, stinking, skinny. Who will love you? Not him. He isn't real, you made him to fill a void, like you made me.

Scattered tools, matted hair, bloodied hands feverishly moulding rough clay. Dark, dense and gritty. The ground remains of others reclaimed. Weirder than usual. Building with bodies. Trancelike I watch you sensuously touch the form, measuring your hands against his. His cheek will never warm to your touch.

I cannot remember when you started, what day it is. You're is lost in this creation. Everywhere are photographs, sketches, ideas, plans, that goddamned photograph. There are little ones, tiny grotesques, a twisted Lilliput. Limbs, fractured torsos, all watching. your audience. Stripped down, sweating from the kilns and drying ovens. Dehydrated and thin in oversized boots. You disgust me. You're weak without me. I'm ashamed of you, and more ashamed that I need you. You're all I have. I'm all you need. Sort your fucking shit out.

*

Bloated and distorted. It took five days to find her. The bespectacled doctor knocking persistently on the door, calling the authorities after peering nosily through the window. White taut skin, protruding ribs, swollen tongue. Clay streaked through her hair like external rigour mortis. Everybody aghast. Fascinated and appalled. Vulgar in their interest. As they went through the notebooks, dog-eared on the table, she came to life more and more. She grew, developed features, a sense of humour that was dark and twisted. Letters to and from, all together, some replies, pleas, forthright demands. Different voices emerged, alternate hand writing, a plethora of pens, colours, drawings. Conversations consisting of pages and personalities. Initially addressed to no one, then suddenly a name. Wendy

No one claimed her.

An Astráil,
Poetry from Australia and New Zealand
with Denise O'Hagan

Editorial

In selecting poetry for this Issue, I was reminded yet again of the particular sort of magic that this art form exerts over us. Poetry is often referred to as being an unveiling of sorts, an emotional letting go, the act of which brings with it a level of transcendence – but equally it is a craft, where form and expression are finely honed and underpinned by intellectual rigour.

In the best poetry, the effect is quite natural. The effort that has been poured into it is invisible, and the whole works together seamlessly; we, the readers, are simply left moved, if not changed, by the experience of reading or hearing it.

The work of the four poets presented in Issue 43 all do this superbly well. Their poetry, varied in subject matter and style, is always lucid, finely crafted, and appeals to both heart and mind.

Our featured poet, **Peter Boyle**, leads us into a territory of deep reflection and, in language both humble and fearless, articulates what many of us fumble towards at some point in our lives, as he speculates in 'Figure in a small icon' that '*If the earth explodes this night / and I am all that is left of humanity / any future sentient being ... / will see only the godhead buried / at every moment within us – / not the deceit, the violence, the greed / that ruled our days.*' 'The parade of moments' of our lives – the title of his second poem – concludes with the exquisite image of a life potentially slipping through a hole in a trouser pocket, memorable in its littleness.

In an act of extraordinary courage and dignity, **Kate McNamara**'s first poem 'To Eamon' pays heartbreaking homage to her 'implacably dead' son, squeezing language to use '*what thin words*' are left to her as she reflects upon how his life '*gleams and leaps somewhere / beyond me, as if / a bright fish dreamt it*'. Her second poem, 'Tree as cosmos', carries with it a suggestion of redemption, where she pauses to '*learn*' the language of trees, '*curator of memory / consecration of time / studded with stars*'.

Frailty and strength are also twin themes of **Davide Angelo**'s powerful portrayal of an 'Open house', where '*glass is an unbreakable honeyed mass, / At its most fragile as it spools and cools into form, invisible / Until it cracks against the wings of* *sparrows'*. If the nature of the ultimate is pondered, so are the beginnings of things; in his second poem, 'Mountain at the end of the world', he reflects, *'There was a time when we were first / spoke the first word / told the first lie, made the first kill / felt the first wave of remorse / only to forget for the first time'*.

Julie Maclean also takes us back to beginnings. Steeped in gentle irony, 'Shark baby Hallelujah' is simultaneously a tribute to the sculptures of a textile artist and to the birth of her child *'Lamb-boy with wings, I want to keep you / but not as a tooth sculpture on a plinth … / You are my pillow-ticking chrysalis … / I finger each of your vertebrae / through the flesh carapace / of my doming womb.'* Her second poem, 'An hour in the gallery of glass', speculates *'Is this what we have become / How we manage the past / Make it beautiful / or leave it buckling among salt bush / and clots of granite / as testament to survival?'*

Please immerse yourself in the poetry of these four exceptional artists, and let them work their magic upon you.

Denise O'Hagan
AUS/NZ Poetry Editor

Featured Poet Peter Boyle

FIGURE IN A SMALL ICON

My royal robe is full of blue crosses.
I am looking at you as if into
an anonymous camera that has commanded me
to lay myself open – my short beard, my
clipped black hair. I have just arrived
or am about to leave, and my royalty
or sainthood or status as marked prisoner
gives me the vulnerability of one
who will be eternally fixed – precisely so.
If the earth explodes this night
and I am all that is left of humanity
any future sentient being
will judge us to have been creatures
given no other means of defence
than the nakedness of their gaze.
They will see only the godhead buried
at every moment within us –
not the deceit, the violence, the greed
that ruled our days.

THE PARADE OF MOMENTS

In the here and now I am restless,
In the here and now I am scattered,
In the here and now it is cold, the sky is a purple tinge of grey and,
        outside, a heavy green foliage blankets the trees,
In the here and now a great distance opens between myself
        and the simplest shape of beauty, of joy.

And yet I have just been meditating,
And yet I have just been sitting, holding tight to breath-awareness,
And yet a moment ago my life lay before me, threaded together
        by long strands of radiance, of certitude,
A moment ago I said, inside myself I am Buddha.

Meanwhile my eyes sting from onions chopped
        half an hour ago,
Meanwhile my head throbs for no reason, slightly, persistently,
Meanwhile I squeeze my eyes shut till a quiet pulsing
        erupts from the still sadness at the earth's core.

And today I have listened to Mahler,
And today I have walked by the river,
And today I have filled pages with words broken loose
        like chipped stones.

It grows cold in the heavy depths of my boots.
Autumn spills quietly into winter.

Today I may be lost
or today I may be stumbling, more sideways than forward,
while daylight's ebb and flow
tilts a little more into darkness.
With no time to assemble them,
messages arrive from the vanishing world.

Today the house is still
and, in my shirt pocket, memory places
the note to collect from the Dry Cleaners the trousers
        with the hole to be mended
in the right pocket where my life might
        any moment slip through.

Poetry by Kate McNamara

TO EAMON

Be not unquiet
my wise dead son,
I'll write your name again
in cobwebs.
You, who are so
implacably dead.

With what thin words
left to me, I'll craft
another epitaph, veins
aching, clawing
at the ravaged, empty past.

And it is no long
journey, no memory
but a maze, hazardous.
It is the travel
of a colourless season.

But your life, so stormy,
gleams and leaps somewhere
beyond me, as if
a bright fish dreamt it.

So I'll hunt the shoreline,
as some eagles would
be black and come alone,
I'll hunt a feather,
think of nothing but the shell.

Fifteen summers, my first love.
Did they make you a man?
O Absalom, Absalom.

TREE AS COSMOS

I have my words
    my talismans
        my shamans

but before you
    out of space
        out of time

I lay down
    your smooth bark
        the curve of your words

as you lie
    sacred in time
        I caress your skin

we speak in air
    in blue leaves hissing
        beneath us your tendrils

weave a trace in time
so old so old
I am young within you

as tiny as a notch
    in your gravid bark
        and I hear you

patient as I speak
your name
Manniferous manifest magnetic

you have your own alphabet
    a syntax of old Gods
        I will learn you

curator of memory
    consecration of time
        studded with stars

stay with me.

Poetry by Davide Angelo

OPEN HOUSE

To tame and cure this trembling house
The owners have lovingly cancelled out the roadway
With whale songs in door hinges, steady Balearic beats
And downtempo deep house soundscapes.
Built in 1950 and meticulously updated by an old friend
Who came to mend a broken affection and smudged
'Unstable elements' with a burning offering of sage
Because surely, someone must have died here.
The house's heart lies at the very end of a long corridor.
The beginning of the universe is buried right under our feet.
If frogs are known as indicator species, take one through
The generous living room as an indicator of future happiness.
We're most vulnerable at both ends of the arrow.
Inside the open fireplace, glass is an unbreakable honeyed mass,
At its most fragile as it spools and cools into form, invisible
Until it cracks against the wings of sparrows.

MOUNTAIN AT THE END OF THE WORLD

'... one of them caught our eye, the one in the centre... heading towards the mountains...'
        Werner Herzog, *Encounters at the End of the World*

The mountain is not indifferent
to our incantations or the slow rumble
of magma that wakes the wilderness' malice.
My eyes are the first in 30,000 years
to see pigment blown over hollow bones
on the cave's face.
Last night I dreamt I carried my own hands.
But why?
The city of gold exists
because we trust our eyes.
There was a time when we were first
spoke the very first word
told the first lie, made the first kill
felt the first wave of remorse
only to forget for the first time.
Who imitated the cicadas first
stole their tymbals, climbed the tree
and made the first drum?
I storyboarded this dream
a jump cut   the signal cycle two rhythms
      of the traffic light
      tick   tick   tick
and the red hand
on the red man
could be the same hand
making art in blood
and memory.
One of them catches my eye
the one in the centre
heading towards the mountain
to the soundtrack of eagle screams
and leopard growls
and like him, I want to live
between actuality and narrative
– humiliating the landscape.
Beating his own breast
drinking from the opened ground
the first monkey climbs him, claims him
as the mountain.

Poetry by Julie Maclean

SHARK BABY HALLELUJAH
after Mister Finch, textile artist

Lamb-boy with wings   I want to keep you
but not as a tooth sculpture on a plinth
posing before vintage bookery or rusting
among machinery of men
where simple stone is gripped
with such a root system
such grunt and muscularity

You and I   stitched together instead
as voile   the ease and sheerness of you
in symbiosis

I harbour you, my sacred parasite
under this canopy of stellar activity
and sonar

You are my pillow-ticking chrysalis
   and when fully formed
      I finger each of your vertebrae
        through the flesh carapace
          of my doming womb
          You are my abacus
         and I am counting down
      Slick grub
   your backbone positively gleams
in your special upholstery

AN HOUR IN THE GALLERY OF GLASS

What to do   in the space left ahead?

Is it enough to wander through
a forest of glass   past paling fences
incised with lines of an older woman
         who might give her secrets away?

A tree of wire grows out of a rusted
wheel hub
Ears of wheat sprout artfully from
corrugations

Is this what we have become
         How we manage the past
         Make it beautiful
         or leave it   buckling among salt bush
         and clots of granite
         as testament to survival?

What to do with the space left inside –
         the glass heart   blue faces
etched somehow into ventricles
and that lotus flower   such resilience

held by   an arcing stem   an aorta almost
         unbreakable   dry eye open to the monsoon
where cumulus assemble
then disperse as those forced to flee
         across the diaspora

How they must ponder liquid light
in an alien sky   the way sand forms
in lunettes and sings of the lost
         and found   the urgency of precipitation –
         the next fall

Contributors
in order of appearance

George Szirtes Born in Hungary in 1948, his first book, *The Slant Door* (1979) won the Faber Prize. He has published many since then, *Reel* (2004) winning the T S Eliot Prize, for which he has been twice shortlisted since. His memoir of his mother, *The Photographer at Sixteen,* was published in February 2019.

Mark Roper is an English poet, living in Ireland for some 40 years now. His latest poetry collection *Bindweed*, Dedalus Press (2017), was shortlisted for The Irish Times Poetry Now Award. *A Gather of Shadow* (2012) was also shortlisted for that Award and won the Michael Hartnett Award in 2014. With photographer Paddy Dwan, he has published *The River Book*, *The Backstrand*, and *Comeragh*.

Eleanor Hooker's third poetry collection *Mending the Light*, and two chapbooks are forthcoming. She holds an MPhil (Distinction) in Creative Writing from Trinity College, Dublin. Her poems have been published in Poetry Ireland Review, POETRY magazine, PN Review, Banshee, The Stinging Fly, Agenda and Poetry Review (forthcoming). Eleanor is a Fellow of the Linnean Society of London. She is a helm and Press Officer for Lough Derg RNLI lifeboat. www.eleanorhooker.com

Luke Kennard is a British poet, critic, novelist and lecturer. He won an Eric Gregory Award in 2005 for his first collection *The Solex Brothers*. His second collection, *The Harbour Beyond The Movie*, was shortlisted for the 2007 Forward Prize for Best Collection, making him the youngest ever poet to be nominated. In 2014 Luke was named as one of the Poetry Book Society's Next Generation Poets. His debut novel, *The Transition*, was published by Fourth Estate in March 2017 and was a BBC Radio 4 *Book at Bedtime*.

Mary Oishi was named Albuquerque Poet Laureate on July 1, 2020. Oishi is the author of *Spirit Birds They Told Me* (West End Press, 2011), and co-author with her daughter, Aja Oishi, of *Rock Paper Scissors* (Swimming with Elephants Publications, 2018), finalist for the New Mexico Arizona Book Award. She is one of twelve U.S. poets in translation in 12 *Poetas: Antologia De Nuevos Poetas Estadounidenses* (La Herrata Feliz and MarEsCierto, 2017), a project of the Mexican Ministry of Culture.

Carolyn Martin's poems and book reviews have appeared in publications throughout North America, Australia, and the UK. Her fourth collection, *A Penchant for Masquerades*, was released by Unsolicited Press in February 2019. Carolyn currently serve as the book review editor for the Oregon Poetry Association and poetry editor of *Kosmos Quarterly: journal for global transformation.*www.carolynmartin.com

Adina Dabija was born in Aiud, Romania. A poet and playwright, she now lives in New York, where she practices oriental medicine. Her first book, poezia-papusa, was awarded the Bucharest Writers' Association Guild Prize. In 2011 she published Beautybeast (North Shore Press), her first collection of poetry in English and in 2012 her first novel, Saman (Polirom).

Jeff Santosuosso is an award-winning poet from Pensacola, FL. His chapbook Body of Water is from Clare Songbirds Publishing House. Jeff's work was nominated for the Pushcart Prize and has appeared in *The Comstock Review, The Lake (UK)* among others.

Pui Ying Wong is the author of two full-length books of poetry: *An Emigrant's Winter* (Glass Lyre Press, 2016) and *Yellow Plum Season* (New York Quarterly Books, 2010) and two chapbooks. She has won a Pushcart Prize. Her poems have appeared in Ploughshares, Prairie Schooner, Crannog among others.

Michael Morpurgo (Sir Michael Andrew Bridge Morpurgo, OBE, FRSL, FKC) is an immensely popular and much-loved author, poet and playwright, although he prefers the term 'story-maker'. Perhaps best-known for 'War Horse', a story which tells of the experiences of Joey, a horse sold to the army in the First World War, Michael Morpurgo has published well over 100 books. He is passionate about the importance of literature as a means of helping you to 'look beyond yourself'.

Sophia Kouidou-Giles, born in Greece, resides in the USA. Her work has appeared in Voices, Persimmon Tree, Assay, The Raven's Perch and The Time Collection. Her poetry chapbook is Transitions and Passages. Her memoir, Επιστροφή Στη Θεσσαλονίκη, published in Greece, is forthcoming by She Writes Press, entitled The Return.

Michael Paul Hogan is a poet, journalist, fiction writer and literary essayist whose work has appeared extensively in the UK, USA, India and China. He is the author of six poetry collections and is currently working on a book of short stories.

Kevin Kling, storyteller/author, lives in Minnesota. His plays have been produced worldwide including off Broadway's Second Stage Theater. He has received numerous awards including the Whiting and an NEA grant and was named the Minneapolis Storyteller Laureate in 2014. He has written five books.

Dominic Fisher has been widely published in magazines and his poems have been broadcast on BBC Radio. In 2018 he was the winner of the Bristol Poetry Prize, and his collection The Ladies and Gentlemen of the Dead was published by The Blue Nib in March 2019.

Cătălina Florina Florescu was born in Romania, graduated "Litere" from University of Bucharest. She earned her PhD in Medical Humanities from Purdue University. She teaches in New York, organizes a theater festival in Jersey City, and travels the world via her fiction, mostly in the dramatic genre. catalinaflorescu.com

Josie Di Sciascio-Andrews is a poet, an author, and a teacher. She has written seven collections of poetry. Her work has been published in many journals and anthologies. Her poems have won several prizes. Josie was born in Italy. She currently lives and writes in Oakville, Ontario, Canada.

Margot Saffer is a South African who came of age as her country emerged from apartheid. Pre-Corona, she was living, writing, and guiding clients on a boat in the ancient Jaffa Port as a body-psychotherapist and astrologer. Her writing has been published in four languages on five continents.

Viviana Fiorentino is Italian and lives in Belfast. She published in international webzines, journals, in anthology (Dedalus Press, 2019); a poetry collection (Controluna Press) and a novel (Transeuropa Publishing House). She co-founded two activist poetry initiatives ('Sky, you are too big', 'Letters with wings') and Le Ortique (forgotten women artists blog).

Mike Farren is the author of two pamphlets: 'Pierrot and his Mother' (Templar) and 'All of the Moons' (Yaffle). He was runner-up in the Blue Nib Chapbook Chapbook Contest IV, judged by Helen Mort. He has been placed in several other competitions and his poems and reviews have appeared widely.

Antony Osgood lives a skimmed-stone's bounce from Margate. His youth involved hauling coals to Newcastle: worked in psychology, autism, disability fields, wrote & edited books, chapters, articles, moved into academia. Retired, he writes full time, and is completing his second novel. He passes his time with little to show for it.

Helen Campbell lives in Dublin. Some years ago, she had plays broadcast on RTE Radio and fiction on BBC Radio 4. Then writing paused as work took over. Currently completing an MA in Creative Writing in DCU, her story Carousel was shortlisted for *Words by Water* in 2019.

Delia Pring enjoys experimentation, toying with the malleable form of the essay to produce work that cannot comfortably reside within a specific category. She contributes regularly to The Write Life and The Blue Nib. She completed her MA in 2019 and lives in Devon.

Peter Boyle is a Sydney-based poet and translator of poetry from Spanish and French. He is the author of eight books of poetry and, in 2020, won the Kenneth Slessor Poetry Prize with his book *Enfolded in the Wings of a Great Darkness*.

Kate McNamara is a Canberra-based poet, playwright and critical theorist. Her plays have been performed internationally. Her published works include *The Void Zone* (1999), *Leaves* (1999) and *Praxis* (1997) (Aberrant Genotype Press), and she is currently writing a memoir, *The Burning Times*. She has worked extensively as an editor and has recently returned to her first love, poetry.

Davide Angelo's poems have appeared in various Australian literary journals. In 2019, he was awarded Second Prize in the Melbourne Poets Union International Poetry Prize and longlisted for the University of Canberra Vice Chancellor's International Poetry Prize.

Julie Maclean has published five collections after a career teaching English and EAL in Australia and in UK. Her collection *When I Saw Jimi* was joint winner of the Geoff Stevens Memorial Poetry Prize (Indigo Dreams Publishing, UK). She lives on the Surf Coast, Victoria. Website: www.juliemacleanwriter.com

The Blue Nib relies on the generosity of subscribers and patrons to produce the magazine and maintain the website at www.thebluenib.com

To become a subscriber, visit our subscription page at
thebluenib.com/the-giving-circle

To order back issues or additional copies of this issue,
visit our publishing partner at Chaffinch Press.
chaffinchpress.com

Made in the USA
Columbia, SC
26 September 2020